Make It Clear

Make It Clear

Speak and Write to Persuade and Inform

Patrick Henry Winston

Foreword by Gill Pratt

The MIT Press
Cambridge, Massachusetts
London, England

This book was set in Sabon LT Std and Frutiger by Patrick Henry Winston and Karen A. Prendergast. Printed and bound in the United States of America.

Library of Congress Cataloging-in-Publication Data is available.

ISBN: 978-0-262-53938-8

10 9 8 7 6 5 4 3 2

Contents

Contents

Part VI Special Cases

Foreword by Gill Pratt

Communication is, without question, the most important enabler of human civilization.

Without our sophisticated ability to communicate, we would still be living in caves, desperately searching for resources, while living in fear of predators.

Every man-made thing, from cars to computers to poetry, results from communication.

And yet, the communication bandwidth between human beings is limited to rates on the order of 10 bits per second of Shannon entropy. This rate is astonishingly low—about the same whether we communicate through voice or through writing. By comparison, even ordinary personal computers today can communicate with one another at a gigabit per second—100 million times faster than human communication.

> You can think of Shannon entropy as the amount of information that results from the most effective possible compression.

How do we overcome our extraordinary communication bandwidth limitation?

We do so by exploiting the subject of this book—our ability to tell stories that evoke imagination.

Whenever a speaker communicates with a listener, the speaker evokes in the listener's mind a picture—a model—of what is being described. The speaker's words guide the listener's model, assembling in their mind complex ideas drawn from the shared heritage and experience of the speaker and listener.

> I use the words *speaker* and *listener* interchangeably with *writer* and *reader*, respectively.

This model-based communication technique serves the function of compression, with the shared heritage and experiences of both parties playing the role of the constellation of code words used in typical computational data compression.

So, part of the art of effective human communications is the art of compressing data to get through an incredibly small 10 bit/s bottleneck.

The other part of effective communication is holding your audience's interest by having a model of their emotional mind, and evoking and steering their emotions with skill.

There have been few practitioners of both parts of this art more intelligent, capable, and kind than this book's author, Patrick Henry Winston.

I knew Patrick for 40 years, from my arrival at MIT as a freshman in 1979 to a few days before his passing in 2019, when I had the good fortune of talking to him about communication one last time. Despite the stark setting of his hospital room and illness, we spoke about many things.

First, how the order of 10 bits/s limit seems to exist even for esoteric modes of human communication, like EEG.

We spoke about how even our visual system may not convey any higher Shannon entropy due to the compression of retinal images into cognitive meaning by the visual cortex. We discussed how several organizations, including DARPA and startups like Neuralink, are exploring whether novel brain interfaces can surpass this limit. We were both skeptical. Perhaps the cognitive part of our brain faces fundamental limits of input/output information bandwidth that render it impossible to easily surpass the efficiency of normal human communication.

We spoke finally about the second part of communication beyond data compression—the art of storytelling and the skill of accurately estimating a listener's state of mind and telling a story in a way to elicit interest. We spoke about how understanding the human mind well enough to draw engagement and focus from one's audience remains a rare, but teachable skill.

Patrick taught many of us this art. We learned it by listening to him lecture, and by listening to him lecture about lecturing.

It is hard to describe the joy of being a student of a great teacher. I had the fortune of having Patrick as my greatest teacher of communication. As is true for many others, I owe Patrick a great deal, and I use the lessons he taught me every day.

I cannot imagine a better teacher of this subject than Patrick, or a better storyteller on the art of storytelling.

You are in for a treat.

Gill Pratt

SB '83, SM '87, PhD '89
Electrical Engineering and Computer Science
Massachusetts Institute of Technology

CEO, Toyota Research Institute

Fellow, Toyota Motor Corporation

Acknowledgments

I am much indebted to Karen Prendergast and Sarah Winston for their myriad suggestions, all of which I accepted, with varying degrees of grace.

Paul Keel and Chiai Takahashi provided many structure, layout, and content suggestions. Gill Pratt generously contributed the Foreword.

Many others offered major suggestions about content. These include: Robert Berwick, Robert Birnbaum, Philippe Brou, Randall Davis, Delores Etter, Mark Finlayson, Kathleen Freeman, Ellen Hildreth, Dylan Holmes, Boris Katz, Kimberle Koile, Adam Kraft, Henry Lieberman, David Martinez, Joel Moses, Peggy Moses, Gerald Jay Sussman, Julie Sussman, Peter Szolovits, Michael Telson, Gaurav Tewari, Hector Vazquez, David Wilcox, Rob Wesson, and Zhutian Yang.

I am especially grateful to Janey Pratt, who provided valuable advice and encouragement.

Prologue: You Will Be Empowered

You will learn how to speak and write well from this book. The return on the time you invest in acquiring knowledge about how to communicate will be bigger than the return on any other investment you make.

In this chapter, you learn that there are principles that apply to all kinds of communication, both spoken and written. If you make use of just one principle from reading this book, that principle may be the life-changing one that gets you the job, wins the award, brings in the grant or contract, makes the sale, convinces your boss, excites the venture capitalist, inspires a student, or starts a revolution.

If you persuade or instruct, speak or write, this book is for you

You persuade and instruct if you work in business, especially in sales and marketing. You persuade and instruct if you train or educate, if you do research in anything from anthropology to zoology, if you are in defense or law enforcement, if you are a student eager to get a good grade, if you preach or run a non-profit organization, and certainly if you practice law, medicine, architecture, or journalism. All these have much in common. All involve moving ideas from you to your audience.

As you persuade and instruct, you will speak and write. Many present with slides or help prepare such presentations. Some lecture, question witnesses, or run for office. Some write scholarly papers, compose position papers, construct legal briefs, or develop business plans. All these have much in common.

You will learn about academic, business, and government communication

When I became a Professor of Artificial Intelligence at MIT, I resolved to study those around me with good communication skills, focusing on what good communicators do that make them good.

As a professor, I listened to and gave lectures, research presentations, conference talks, and task-force reports. As an author,

I wrote and edited books on programming languages, Artificial Intelligence, and the business of Artificial Intelligence. As a laboratory director, I wrote proposals and learned to sell research programs. As a member of government science advisory boards, I watched countless briefs on all sorts of subjects, and I learned how to assemble actionable recommendations valued by government sponsors. As an entrepreneur, I interacted with venture capitalists and learned what they value in presentations.

I learned a lot. I learned by making mistakes. I learned by experimenting. But mostly I learned because I observed and studied great communicators and listened to knowledgeable critics. When you read this book, you will learn what took me decades to learn from those great communicators and knowledgeable critics, including not only colleagues, authors, researchers, students, journalists, editors, sponsors, lawyers, military officers, politicians, business people, and investors, but also artists, architects, chefs, designers, musicians, theologians, and many more in between.

You will learn communication essentials

What you learn about one kind of speaking and writing will make you better at all kinds of speaking and writing. Here are a few representative things I do or help students to do:

- Present research at a conference.
- Write a paper for a technical journal.
- Lecture to hundreds of listeners.
- Develop a funding proposal.
- Explain results to a business audience.
- Send a call to arms in a letter to an editor.
- Give an after-dinner talk at an awards dinner.
- Talk through a poster or board.
- Write a review.
- Write a recommendation.
- Survive a thesis defense.
- Deliver a job-interview talk.

Skill in such activities is broadly applicable to other communication challenges such as you encounter when you have to:

- Present a business idea to a venture capitalist.
- Sell a product to a customer.
- Present a development plan to a manager.
- Express the findings of a consulting engagement.
- Deliver the recommendations of a study group.
- Brief senior people who are unfamiliar with your field.
- Organize a panel discussion.
- Compose an opinion piece.
- Work with an interviewer.
- Inspire those with whom you work.

Experiences with challenges such as these have led me to believe that what you learn about one kind of speaking and writing will make you better at all kinds of speaking and writing.

You start learning about elements common to all kinds of speaking and writing in Part I of this book as I introduce key ideas. I build upon those key ideas in subsequent parts of the book that focus on presentation, instruction, writing, design, and special cases. Eventually, you should read the entire book, but you can start with those parts that address your immediate needs.

You will find your own voice

I was 10,000 meters or so up in the air and bored stiff. I picked up an airline magazine, and there it was, in an interview of Ingemar Stenmark, arguably the greatest slalom and giant slalom skier ever, some of the best advice I ever got.

The interviewer asked Stenmark how he came to be so good. Stenmark answered that he watched other skiers, analyzed what they did, and adapted some of what he observed to suit his body and overall style.

While reading this book, you will be like Stenmark, analyzing my advice and adapting some of it to your own developing style. Then, once you see that there are principles that can make you a more effective communicator, you will look for them everywhere. When you hear good speaking and when you read good writing, you will ask yourself why you think the speaking or writing is good and whether you have found a principle you want to adapt to your own developing style. You will, as my friends in the humanities like to say, find your own voice.

Because I offer many principles in this book, it would be hard to find another person who agrees with all of them. Just keep this in mind: some speakers and some writers are great even though they violate some of the offered principles. No good speaker or writer violates them all.

You will be smarter

As you learn how to organize your communications, you will learn how to organize your thoughts, identify strengths and weaknesses, and focus effort on what matters. You also will learn how to identify and remember the essential elements in the communications you hear and read.

Promise

- You will learn how to speak and write well from this book.
- You will be richly rewarded for the time you spend reading it.

For more on empowerment promise, see page 143.

For more on promise delivery, see page 152.

You will learn, for example, that you should start instruction with an empowerment promise and conclude by noting you have delivered on that empowerment promise. In this Prologue, I make empowerment promises. In the Epilogue, page 319, I note I have delivered.

Part I
Essentials

Your success likely will be determined by how well you speak, by how well you write, and by the quality of your ideas, in that order.

Patrick Henry Winston; American computer scientist, professor, and writer

1 Essentials of Persuasion

In this chapter, you learn principles applicable to communication whenever your purpose is to persuade your listeners and readers to think favorably of you, your idea, or your product. You may want them to hire you, honor you, find your idea interesting, make a better decision, believe your idea is the right way, or buy your product.

In particular, you learn how to start and stop spoken presentations and written work so as to ensure you are heard and read. In *Essentials for Being Remembered* (page 15), you learn principles for being remembered once you are heard and read.

Show your hand immediately

I spent a lot of time in San Diego, CA, as a member of the US Naval Research Advisory Committee (NRAC), a legacy name for a board that advised the US Department of the Navy about science and technology. One day, I was at the Fish Market Restaurant with William Weldon, a Professor from the University of Texas, and Delores Etter, a Professor from the University of Colorado, also members of NRAC.

Somehow the conversation turned to hiring new faculty. It was my great good luck to ask, "What do you look for in a job-interview talk?" Delores said and Bill instantly agreed, "The candidate has to show us they have some sort of vision and they have done something about it."

"How long do they have to get that across?" I asked. Bill answered this one, "Not more than five minutes."

Five minutes! That means you cannot develop your talk like a symphony, holding back your big idea and stupendous results for a big crescendo at the end. Instead, you must show your hand right away.

And what is true for a job-interview talk is also true for any spoken presentation of your ideas. You have at most only a few minutes to convince people to listen to you. If you do not show them that you or your organization have a vision and have done something about it, they may sit there, but they will fog out, thinking about what to have for lunch or responding to text messages.

It is even worse for written work: busy readers will devote not more than a few seconds to deciding whether to read about your ideas.

Use the VSN-C framework

So that audiences and readers will see that you have a vision and know that you have done something about it, you need a framework that helps you start and stop. When speaking and writing, I use what I call the Vision–Steps–News··· Contributions framework, frequently abbreviated to VSN-C. You start with a quick statement of your Vision; next you enumerate the Steps you have been taking; and then you supply News by describing something that just happened. You finish with an enumeration of your Contributions.

Thus, the bulk of your talk, the exposition part, lies between your Vision, Steps, and News on the front end and your Contributions on the back end.

The Vision–Steps–News··· Contributions framework is a foundation for all sorts of spoken and written communication.

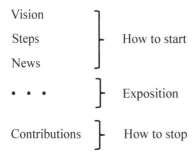

Vision
Steps } How to start
News

• • • } Exposition

Contributions } How to stop

Start with your Vision

Your Vision combines a problem people care about and an approach to that problem's solution. It is necessary, but not sufficient, to care about the problem yourself. You need to be sure your audience also cares.

Express a community-specific vision

Once, I did a trial run of a talk I was to give to Naval officers at the Naval War College in Newport, RI. I thought my talk was fascinating; it was all about using Artificial Intelligence to advance the practice of signal processing. Gerald A. Cann, Assistant Secretary of the Navy, did not think so. "Too academic," he said. I got the point and quickly rearranged the talk around what the officers would care about, namely a threat to a Naval mission and a new idea about how to deal with the threat. I no longer had a Vision centered on signal processing; my Vision centered on detecting submarines.

If you are a technology entrepreneur or a venture capitalist, your problem is to identify new ways to make money. You are likely to pay attention to a speaker who offers a plan to start a company to build and sell general-purpose robots that make low-cost copies of themselves.

If you are the vice president of manufacturing in a large corporation, your problem may be to identify new ways to reduce costs. You are likely to pay attention to a speaker who offers a solution to rapidly escalating costs via low-cost, productivity-amplifying robots.

If you are an academic, you are curious by nature, and hence interested in anything interesting, but you are most interested in your own field and its unsolved problems. You are likely to pay attention to a speaker who identifies one of those unsolved problems and offers a new way to look at it.

Use a community-specific title

Should you title your Vision slide *Vision*? You can, but sometimes a community-specific title is better. There are several that you can think of as synonyms, such as, for example, *Threat*, *Opportunity*, *Goal*, and *Hypothesis*.

For more on community expectations, see page 171.

Enumerate your Steps

Once you have convinced everyone that you have a Vision—a problem and an approach to solving it—you need to convince everyone that you have done something about it. To be convincing, you start by exhibiting a carefully thought-out plan. Then, you demonstrate your intellectual athleticism by showing that you have made progress on at least one of the Steps in the plan.

Note that your Steps exhibit is not necessarily a history of what you have done. You need not recite, for example, minor steps, obvious steps, or steps that proved to be dead ends. The point is to show you think about what you are doing. As President Dwight D. Eisenhower noted in a speech to the National Defense Executive Reserve Conference, "Plans are worthless, but planning is everything" (Eisenhower, 1957).

You do not have to have completed all the Steps when you apply for a faculty position or a research job. In fact, you should emphasize that the next exciting Step in your plan will take place at the fortunate organization whose offer you accept. After all, no one wants to hire someone who will be devoted to polishing up work done at another place.

When you apply for a business job, however, the question is not whether you are ready to do something new, but rather whether you can replicate your successes. Stick to Steps you have finished.

Announce News

The Step you have just completed constitutes News because you have just completed it. Announce it with fanfare. Show what you have done right up front, and explain that the rest of your oral presentation or written work will show how you did it.

You do this to assure your audience that you are not describing old work. Your presentation or writing is about right now, about today's excitement, about your passion, about what will happen tomorrow and next week. Your audience will feel privileged to learn about it before everyone else.

Continue with the body of your talk

For more on outlining, see page 30.

Once you have articulated your Vision, shown your Steps, and announced News, then you enter the body of your talk where you explain what you have done in detail, guided by what you have accumulated when outlining your talk.

You should consider breaking up the body of your talk into enumerated parts. That way, you provide places where you can summarize and where those whose attention has strayed can reengage.

For more on enumerated parts, see page 112.

Each community has community expectations. If you are giving a technical talk, for example, your community may expect slides with titles such as, for example, *Problem statement*, *Methods*, *Results*, *When it works and why*, and *When it fails and why*.

For more on community expectations, see page 171.

Conclude with Contributions

Because you want to persuade your listeners and readers that you have done something, you should always conclude a slide-based talk with a slide titled *Contributions*. A slide bearing only the words *Thank You* persuades no one about anything.

Similarly, you should always conclude your written work with a section titled *Contributions*, or a suitable synonym, that summarizes, in a memorable way, what you or your organization contributed to engineering prowess, scientific research, business acumen, military readiness, non-profit achievement, or other work.

For more on synonyms for *Contributions*, see page 74.

No one is persuaded by a slide or section titled *Conclusions* if it just rambles on about how hard the problem is, or who else has worked on it, or what you might do next.

What you need to know

Whenever your purpose is to persuade, as in to convince audiences and readers to think favorably about you, your idea, your work, or your product, you should be sure to honor essentials of persuasion:

- Show your hand immediately.
- Start with your Vision: identify the problem worth solving and your approach to solving that problem.
- Explain the Steps you are taking to realize your Vision.
- Excite with some News, often about a recent, impressive Contribution.

- Put the body of your talk after your introductory *Vision*, *Steps*, and *News* slides and before the concluding *Contributions* slide. Consider breaking up the body of your talk into enumerated parts.

- Conclude with an enumeration of your most important Contributions, explicitly, in a slide titled *Contributions* or a section titled *Contributions*. Synonyms for *Contributions* include *Recommendations*, *Business messages*, *Assured benefits*, *Projected earnings*, and *What your gift will do*, but never *Conclusions*.

Where you can learn more

For more on presentation, see Carmine Gallo's book, *Talk Like TED: The 9 Public-Speaking Secrets of the World's Top Minds* (Gallo, 2015). It features stories about successful, much watched TED talks.

You get used to it.

Julia Child; American chef, writer, and television personality

Reply when asked by Patrick Henry Winston, over dinner, "Is it fun to be famous?"

2 Essentials for Being Remembered

In *Essentials of Persuasion* (page 7) you learned that the VSN-C framework ensures that you are heard and read. In this chapter, you learn five ways to ensure that your spoken presentations and written work are remembered. Subsequent chapters in Part I address how you can ensure you are understood.

Include a slogan

Ask anyone what they remember about someone's spoken or written communication. If they remember anything, with high probability the answer will be in the form of a short, slogan-like word or phrase that serves as a kind of handle.

In my field, Artificial Intelligence, you might remember: Oh, that's the person who talked about *subsumption architecture*, or *back propagation*, or *merge operation*.

Sometimes, the slogan is the name of a system: Oh, yes, that's the person who led the work on *Genesis*, the story-understanding system, or *Watson*, the Jeopardy-playing program.

You should decide on a suitable slogan for your work and be sure everyone knows what that slogan is. In an oral presentation, you can emphasize your slogan by saying explicitly, "The key idea in my work—the idea I want you to remember—is the power of ⟨*slogan*⟩." In written work, you can put your slogan in your title, abstract, beginning, and end, and in a conspicuous section titled *The key idea: ⟨slogan⟩*.

Include a symbol

Symbols also serve as handles on work. Edward Tufte's *The Visual Display of Quantitative Information* (2001) includes a discussion of Charles-Joseph Minard's famous graphic showing what happened when Napoleon invaded Russia. Minard's graphic has become a kind of symbolic handle for Tufte's book.

Minard's graphic of Napoleon's march in and out of Russia, teaches much, including the shrinking size of Napoleon's army. From Minard (1869).

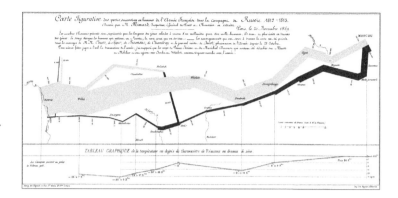

Pictures, drawings, maps, graphs, and graphics can serve as symbols, as suggested by the following examples.

Cynthia Breazeal's emotion-evoking robot, Kismet. From Breazeal (2001). Image courtesy of Cynthia Breazeal.

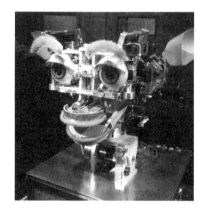

The surprising power of Google's picture-captioning system, NIC, based on deep neural nets. From Vinyals et al. (2014). Image courtesy of Oriol Vinyals.

A group of young people playing a game of frisbee

Some symbols work in harness with a slogan. In the following example, the symbol is the arch and the slogan is *one-shot learning*.

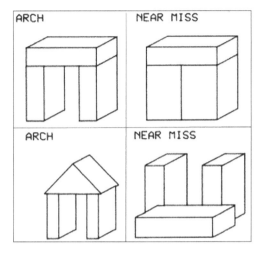

Winston's concept-learning program learned something definite about arches from each example via one-shot learning. It learned, from the first example, the general idea; from the second, the sides cannot touch; from the third, the top can be wedge shaped; and from the fourth, there must be support relations. From Winston (1970).

I exploit the *near-miss* concept frequently throughout this book to reinforce what to do and what not to do in your spoken and written communication. I mark examples of near misses with an icon like this ⊘ in the margin.

Include a salient idea

Surprisingly, a presentation can have too many good ideas. Most people can remember only a few, typically not more than three.

Accordingly, in your talks and writings, you should make one, two, or three ideas explicitly salient. By *salient idea*, I mean an idea that sticks out, not just an important idea. Otherwise, people may remember you as having a lot of ideas, but that is not as good as remembering you as the owner of a particular idea.

How do you signal that a particular idea is the salient idea? You say so, preferably in a few words or sentences.

Slogans are often labels for your salient idea, so the slogan may appear inside your expression of the salient idea. Here is how I would express the salient ideas in papers by various authors:

- Shannon (1948): Each communication channel has a *channel capacity*, and if you are willing to transmit at that rate or lower, there exists an information coding that will allow error-free transmission.

- Watson and Crick (1953): Deoxyribonucleic acid is a *double helix* in which the two strands are connected by adenine-thymine and cytosine-guanine pairs.

- Krizhevsky et al. (2012): Modern computing resources make it possible to construct *deep neural nets* with tens of millions of parameters, and that is enough to turn a curiosity of the 1970s into a world-changing technology 40 years later.

- Berwick and Chomsky (2016): We humans are different from other species because we alone can perform the *merge* operation, which enables us to construct complex, deeply-nested descriptions.

- Winston and Holmes (2018): The merge operation of Berwick and Chomsky matters because merge enables complex descriptions of relations and events, and when we use those descriptions to *create, tell, and understand stories*, our intelligence rises to a level higher than that of our primate cousins.

Include a surprise

We all love surprises. We tell people about them at dinner. We tell people about them again in small talk at parties. So if your work has a surprise in it somewhere, be sure to note it. Here is how I would express the surprises in papers by various authors:

- Winston (1970): The surprise in this work is that a program can learn something definite from each example by noting differences between an evolving model and a near-miss example.

- Brooks (1991): The surprise in this work is that an insect-level robot needs no internal model of the world to avoid obstacles, wander around, explore an area, and seek a particular place.

- Nguyen et al. (2014): The surprise in this work is that deep neural nets can be fooled by images that to us look nothing like the category identified.

- Winston (2018): The surprise in this work is that a story-processing program can tell its own story and process that story, giving the program a kind of self-awareness.

Include a story

Throughout this book, I emphasize that we humans love stories. We want to know not only about ideas and results, but also about who developed them and how. Why did she start to work on the problem? With whom did he work? How did they interact with each other? Was it in the office at a blackboard or strolling along a beach? Did they lose sleep? How long were they stuck? Was there an epiphanous moment? Did someone have a dream? What do they think will happen next?

How to Speak

Here, for example, is how this book came to be written. It started with an accidental conversation several decades ago. I was sitting in my office with a graduate student, Robert Sjoberg, whining about a horrible lecture I had just endured.

Bob said, "You should do a talk on how to speak during MIT's Independent Activities Period."

"No," I said, "I've never given a talk I rate at better than a B+; I would be upset about my performance for a month afterward; it would take a week to prepare; and besides, nobody would come."

"I'll come," he said.

Somehow, that was persuasive, so I started thinking about what I had learned about speaking from various experts, starting when I was myself an MIT undergraduate.

- From David Peterson, I learned to use verbal punctuation.
- From A. R. Gurney, I learned the power of props.
- From Amar Bose, I learned to forbid distractions.
- From Walle Nauta, I learned to draw practiced diagrams.
- From Marvin Minsky, I learned the importance of passion.
- From Randall Davis, I learned to start with a promise.
- From Gerald Jay Sussman, I learned the power of names for things.
- And from a host of others, I learned about what to avoid.

Actually, that first *How to Speak* talk drew about a hundred listeners, so I kept going, and now the talk has become an MIT tradition, with several hundred attending each year.

The annual *How to Speak* talk in the Center of the Universe, MIT Room 10-250. Image courtesy of Chiai Takahashi.

The Tale of Torn Tendons

Then, about 20 years ago, I decided to introduce a new MIT subject, *The Human Intelligence Enterprise*, focused on reading original papers and discussing them. We talk about everything from early papers by Turing and Minsky to work not yet published.

We discuss communication principles, some drawn from the *How to Speak* talk, as well as technical content. We talk about speaking, writing, grant proposals, opinion pieces, business evaluations, how to make decisions, how to persuade, and how to inform.

From time to time, mostly because of student hounding, I thought about capturing some of what we talk about in a book, but I was always too busy.

Then, something unfortunate happened: I managed to tear my quadriceps tendons off my knee caps when I tripped on a step. I like to think of it as a sports-related accident because it happened at the end of a long run.

After my tendons were reattached, I was stuck for weeks in impressive leg braces in a hospital bed. I was bored beyond description because I could not sit in front of my big screens and program.

Then one day it occurred to me I could work up a book outline on the back of a page of my physical therapy instructions. Next, I scribbled out a few fragments on a laptop, thinking I would use them, if for nothing else, as notes for *The Human Intelligence Enterprise* class. By the time I was back sitting in front of my big screens, 150 pages had emerged. I started thinking there might be enough material for a book, and, eventually, my tendons healed, and the 150 pages grew into this silver lining.

Ensure that you are remembered with Winston's star

A well-crafted and explicitly identified Slogan, Symbol, Salient idea, Surprise, and Story combine to make you and your work more memorable. Conveniently, all five elements have labels that start with *S*, making them easier, at least for me, to remember. They form the points on what some people call Winston's star:

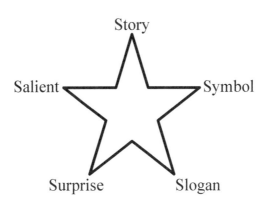

Five elements every presentation and paper should have.

Note that this chapter conspicuously contains all the elements of Winston's star. *Winston's star* is the Slogan. The star image is the Symbol. The Surprise is that you can make your work much more memorable without much effort. The Salient idea is that all you need do is add the elements in the star. The *How to Speak* and *The Tale of Torn Tendons* stories provide human interest and connections to experience.

For more on *How to Speak*, see page 19.

For more on *The Tale of Torn Tendons*, see page 312.

What you need to know

You and your work make a more lasting impression if you include five elements that make your work more memorable:

- Highlight a pithy Slogan.
- Include an iconic Symbol.
- Identify a Surprise.
- Point out a Salient idea.
- Tell a Story.

We are, as a species, addicted to story.

Jonathan Gottschall; American educator and writer

From *The Storytelling Animal: How Stories Make Us Human* (Gottschall, 2012), page xiv

3 Essentials of Instruction

In this chapter, you learn essential points of strategy for instruction. These essential points of strategy will make you more effective in both classrooms and books. In *Essentials of Persuasion* (page 7), you learn essential points of strategy for spoken and written persuasion. There is, of course, much overlap.

Start with an empowerment promise

If you are instructing, you should tell your students what they will be able to do or want to do after they listen to you speak or read what you write. Here is an example for the book and another for the chapter:

> You will learn how to speak and write well from this book. The return on the time you invest in acquiring knowledge about how to communicate will be bigger than the return on any other investment you make.

> In this chapter, you learn essential points of strategy for instruction. These essential points of strategy will make you more effective in both classrooms and books.

Tell stories

We are storytelling animals. In fact, our ability to tell, understand, and compose stories distinguishes the human species from all other animals, living and no longer living. That is why, in my Artificial Intelligence work, I focus on developing an account of our human ability to create, tell, and understand stories.

Jonathan Gottschall, a humanist, agrees that our story competences make us different. In his book titled, fittingly, *The Storytelling Animal: How Stories Make Us Human*, he notes that stories are like flight simulators for real life. He starts every chapter, unsurprisingly, with a story (Gottschall, 2012).

Gottschall notes that when there is no explanation, we tend to make one up, because we are an explanation-seeking species.

Stories have more impact than statistics. Do you want to deter a teenager from smoking? Forget the statistics; tell a story about someone suffering from emphysema. Include illustrations.

Stories are everywhere

In many fields, instruction means analyzing case studies. Law, business, and medicine come to mind, but those are just three of many disciplines characterized by story-based instruction.

- We teach law, business, and medicine via case studies.
- We tell children about danger, good, and evil via fairy tales.
- We convey aspects of culture via the folk tales of the culture.
- We give religious instruction via parables.
- We expose the human condition via literature.
- We shed light on human and societal tendencies via biography and history.

You might think science and engineering are exceptions, but they are not. My colleague Gerald Jay Sussman knows a lot about circuit design, one of his many talents. When he talks about a circuit, he tells a story about how a signal passes through all the components. It is as if the circuit diagram were a kind of storyboard.

Explaining a circuit, viewed as telling a story. A signal enters from the left, goes through capacitor C_{in}, presents itself at the base of transistor $Q1_a$, ... Image courtesy of Gerald Jay Sussman.

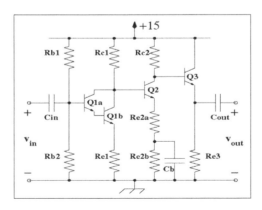

Stories teach principles and methods

Consider the do-not-plagiarize principle. Myriad stories demonstrate the folly of plagiarism. Checking is easy, and the guilty, if they rise to importance, always get caught. When I teach the principle, I tell a few plagiarism stories to illustrate and emphasize the point.

What about skills such as document processing or automobile repair? Many such skills amount to following various recipes, and following recipes is a special case of retelling a story.

Stories teach you how to think

Ask any instructor what is the most important thing he or she teaches. Chances are, the reply will be, "How to think." But how do you teach someone how to think? The answer: by telling stories that serve as precedents for dealing with the future. The American Revolutionary War patriot, Patrick Henry, emphasized the point in one of the most famous speeches of all time, the *Give me liberty or give me death* speech to the Second Virginia Convention on March 23, 1775:

> I have but one lamp by which my feet are guided; and that is the lamp of experience. I know of no way of judging of the future but by the past. (Copeland and Lamm, 1973)

If you are teaching, you do your students a great favor if you not only tell them what to do, but also tell them the story of how the ideas developed. Bring the story alive by noting the characteristics of the people involved. Were they visionary, persistent, and passionate, or just lucky? Were they geniuses? Did they have sharp edges? Did they work it all out on a Saturday afternoon or only after years of struggle?

Deliver on your promise

Once you have made a promise, you need to deliver, and once you have delivered, you should say so. You should say so explicitly because your students may not infer that you have delivered. In a class, you might say something analogous to the following:

- So there you have it; you know why the full moon looks flat.
- So there you have it; you know how to turn lead into gold.
- So there you have it; you know how to get elected.

Written instruction also should note that you have delivered on an up-front empowerment promise. That is why each chapter in this book starts with an empowerment promise and ends with an empowerment-identifying section titled, "What you need to know." That also is why I titled the Prologue, "You Will Be Empowered," and the Epilogue, "You Are Empowered."

What you need to know

So there you have it, you know you should start with an empowerment promise, you understand why stories are important, and you know you should stop by noting that you have delivered on your promise.

I have delivered on my empowerment promise because I have explained how you can be a better instructor and increased your likelihood of inspiring your students.

- You should start each instruction unit—class or chapter—with an empowerment promise.
- You should be sure to note that you have delivered on your promise.
- You should tell stories because we humans love stories and because stories are the center of education at all levels.

4 Essentials of Outlining

In this chapter, you learn how to work up an outline in preparation for all types of communication. In particular, you learn problems associated with a formal outline, and you learn how to deploy a broken-glass outline, which is easier to work with and much more effective.

You could make a formal outline

To structure what you want to say or write, you can make a formal outline, sometimes called a Harvard outline, which specifies a hierarchical structure:

> I. A major division
>   A. A major subdivision
>   1. A minor subdivision
>   2. Another minor subdivision
>   B. Another major subdivision
> II. Another major division
>   A. A major subdivision in the second major division
>   B. Another major subdivision in the second major division

Here is how such an outline would look if I had decided to make one in preparation for writing this book:

> I. Essentials
>   A. This book will empower you
>   1. If you persuade and instruct, this book is for you
>   2. If you speak and write, this book is for you
>   3. ...
>   B. How to be persuasive
>   C. ...
> II. ...

When the Harvard outline is taught, instructors often issue stern warnings: You must follow each Roman numeral, each capital letter, and each Arabic numeral with a period. You cannot have one subdivision; there must be at least two. If you need more nesting, use lower-case letters for the next level.

Before personal computers became common, constructing such an outline was incredibly painful because, when using a typewriter, you had to start over if you felt compelled to insert something.

You should make a broken-glass outline

Rigidity chokes creativity. When you prepare a Harvard outline, you may find yourself wasting time worrying about whether an item should be at the Roman, capital, or Arabic level. And what if you get the urge to work on an outline while stretched out on the beach or over coffee in a cafe with no laptop in sight?

What you need is what I call a *broken-glass outline*, my label for a visualization, similar to a mind map, that looks a bit like broken glass. You start with your title in the center, and then you draw radiating spokes for the major subdivisions. Out of those radiating spokes come more lines for the minor subdivisions.

Here is what the outline of the *Essentials of Instruction* (page 25) chapter looked like when I first prepared it.

First attempt at a broken-glass outline for the *Essentials of Instruction* (page 25) chapter.

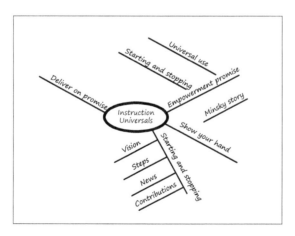

I let it rest overnight. I did not like it in the morning, so I started making changes.

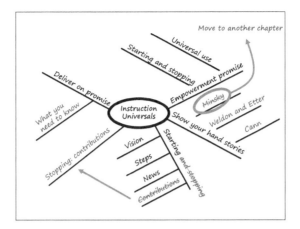

Second attempt at a broken-glass outline for the *Essentials of Instruction* (page 25) chapter.

Note the strike outs and commentary. In the strike outs, I have a history of recent changes. In the commentary, I easily mark an element for a particular kind of action. I move elements around with arrows. I have no investment in Roman numerals, letters, and Arabic numerals, so there is no barrier to change.

Start with standard spokes

From the discussion in the *Essentials of Persuasion* (page 7) chapter, you know that you can start with four standard spokes, each of which will become a slide if you are speaking with slides. Once you finish those four, if you are preparing a 20-minute presentation, you will have about 40% of your slides done.

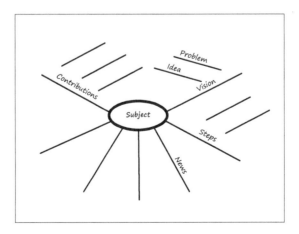

The four primary persuasion spokes: Vision, Steps, News, and Contributions, with lines for minor subdivisions.

Similarly, from the *Essentials of Instruction* (page 25) discussion, you know that your class or chapter will have standard spokes for starting, stories, and stopping.

The three standard instruction spokes: Empowerment promise, Stories, and Deliver on promise.

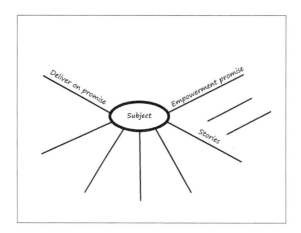

Add detail

For more on active verbs, see page 74.

With the overall structure in place, you begin to add detail. For the Vision spoke in a persuasion talk, you identify the problem and the ideas involved in your approach. For the Steps, you recall what you have done. For the News, you pick some impressive recent result. For the Contributions, you articulate what you have contributed, exercising active verbs such as *hypothesized*, *developed*, and *showed*.

Then, you work on the other spokes, some of which will echo your Steps. You may choose to work depth first, adding spokes down several levels in one place. You may work breadth first, adding spokes at the next level to existing spokes everywhere. You may cross out, comment, add reordering lines, or detach and reattach. You may erase or start over.

If the structure becomes unbalanced, you see it, make adjustments, and eventually, bring everything into balance.

If you are feeling artistic, you can annotate with colored pencil. If you want to work on it with another person or a group, you can work on a board. It is flexible. It works. It is a practical solution.

Maybe it will come to be called the MIT outline.

Drawing makes you smarter

When you draw, you actuate your human visual-thinking faculty. You see how your ideas fit together and flow into one another. By exercising visual thinking, you discover ideas that you did not know you had. One of them may displace what you thought to be your main idea.

Traveling out the spokes of a broken-glass outline helps you recall how your ideas have developed, as when a sketch becomes a painting.

Once your broken-glass outline looks right, then you can make a Harvard outline if you want one.

Broken-glass outlines can help you learn

So far, you have learned that a broken-glass outline helps you prepare to persuade or instruct. Building such an outline can also help you to understand what you hear or read and to remember the most important points. Standard spokes tell you what to look for, as in this illustration by Zhutian Yang.

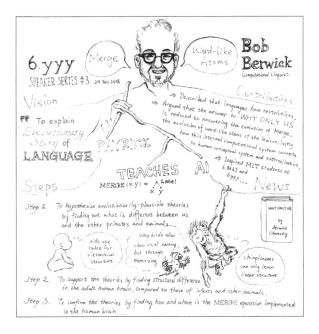

A broken-glass outline captures key points from a classroom question-and-answer session with Robert Berwick. Image courtesy of Zhutian Yang.

For more on how telling yourself a story helps you learn and remember, see page 25.

By arranging and populating standard spokes, you tell yourself a story and telling yourself a story helps you learn and remember.

Broken-glass outlines can help you create

You can use something like a broken-glass outline not only for arranging your ideas and taking notes, but also for creative exploring. Clustering, mind mapping, and idea mapping are names for methodologies that use visualizations much like a broken-glass outline to stimulate creative thinking.

What you need to know

- Use a flexible, easily revised broken-glass outline to avoid the rigidity and awkward imperatives of a formal outline.
- For persuasion, a broken-glass outline generally includes four key spokes, one each for the Vision, Steps, News, and Contributions.
- For instruction, a broken-glass outline generally includes three key spokes, one each for the empowerment promise, stories to be told, and the delivery on the promise.

Criticism may not be agreeable, but it is necessary. It fulfils the same function as pain in the human body; it calls attention to the development of an unhealthy state of things. If it is heeded in time, danger may be averted; if it is suppressed, a fatal distemper may develop.

Winston S. Churchill; British statesman, writer, and Prime Minister

From an interview in the 7 January 1939 issue of *New Statesman Magazine* (Martin, 2013)

5 Essentials of Critiquing

In this chapter, you learn how to select and instruct reviewers for all kinds of communication. You also learn how to give useful criticism.

Select and sequence your reviewers carefully

Some speakers want to surprise friends, colleagues, and judges on presentation day; some writers never invite criticism. Would these speakers and writers try to learn to play music without a teacher or compete in a sport without a coach?

To become a better persuader and instructor, you need to have your speaking and writing criticized. Even teachers and coaches need teachers and coaches.

Do not, however, solicit help exclusively from friends who already know what you have done. The problem is that such friends will imagine that your talk or paper contains explanations that are not actually included.

Also, you should do your practice and endure your criticism sequentially, one friend at a time. Otherwise everyone notes and focuses on the obvious flaws that mask the subtler flaws. Fix the obvious flaws first, then move on to the next friend.

Do not ask for brutal honesty

Friends, especially close friends and relatives, too often excuse presentation flaws. Friends do not like to hurt friends' feelings.

One way to work around the friend problem is to instruct your friends to be brutally honest because you do not want to make mistakes when it counts.

Alas, asking friends to be brutally honest does not provide much guidance. Following it, a friend could abuse you for something you cannot fix, leaving you disheartened and ready to quit. Fortunately, there is a better way.

Ask for maximum return on energy expended

There was a time when *Made in Japan* meant *This is Junk*. Then, just after World War II, General Douglas McArthur brought W. Edwards Deming to Japan to fix the Japanese economy, and Deming helped transform Japan from a maker of junk into the industrial envy of the world. The Japanese Union of Scientists and Engineers has awarded the Deming Prize annually ever since in his honor.

Deming's book, *Out of the Crisis* (1986), is full of good advice collected into a management philosophy that has come to be labeled *Total Quality Management* (TQM). Deming emphasizes, for example, that annual reviews should not be for grading, they should be for identifying what is done well and where improvement would have the most impact. He notes that people need coaches, not scorekeepers.

Much the same can be said for communication reviews. You might think to ask your friends for help via a grading form that ranks you in all sorts of dimensions.

⊘ Do not use such a form. If given one, refuse to use it.

Evaluation
A B C D Knowledgeable
A B C D Understandable
A B C D Authoritative
A B C D Energetic
A B C D Warm
A B C D Relaxed
...

Unfortunately, a grade does not tell you what to do to improve. Also, you might put a lot of energy into bringing a certain grade up from a D when what you really should work on is turning an especially important B into an A.

Instead of providing a grading form, ask your friends to think about what you need to do to make your talk or paper better. So, no grading form. Just ask, "How can I get the maximum improvement on energy expended?"

Asking the maximum-improvement question is not an invitation for ego destruction. It is a question every speaker, even the best, should ask. It is an easy question for a friend to answer because it involves improvement, not evaluation.

So phrased, the maximum-improvement question not only asks your friends to identify the best dimensions for improvement, it also asks what specifically you need to do. It is not a matter of whether you get an A or a D in the passion dimension; it is instead a matter of how you can express more passion, perhaps by sprinkling into your talk a few phrases such as "…and that, I think, is really, really exciting," said, of course, with excitement in your voice.

You also can supply some guidance on where attention should be focused, as in the following:

- Watch for any use of filler words.
- Watch for any instances of up talking.
- Note if I seem excited and passionate about what I do.

For more on filler words, see page 120.

For more on up talking, see page 121.

Without such guidance, your friends might not think to focus on aspects of your talk or paper that are especially important to you.

You might also give your friends a quiz afterward to see if what you tried to do actually worked.

- What is my vision?
- What did I just now accomplish?
- What are my most important contributions?

Offer actionable, principled, positive advice

When you offer advice, remember that you are not trying to prove that you are smarter or better educated than the recipient of your advice. Your purpose is to help a friend or colleague to improve their speaking or writing via maximum improvement on energy expended.

Three conclusions follow:

- Your advice should be actionable, that is, your advice should be in the form of something to do, not a statement that something needs to be improved.
- Your advice should be principled, that is, your advice should not only suggest what to do but also why it should be done.
- Your advice should be positive, that is, the recipient of your advice should feel empowered and energized, not discouraged.

Saying "Your final slide stinks!" provides no actionable, principled, positive elements. Say this instead:

> You can make your talk a lot better without much more effort [positive] by listing your contributions on the final slide [actionable], because that way the slide that is shown longer than any other slide will help to persuade your audience that you have done important work [principled].

Offer criticism at the right time

When asked when it is best to criticise a presentation, many say, without reflection, right after the presentation.

Right-after criticism is fine for content because such criticism can provide guidance, and maybe even stimulation. But for criticism on how the content has been presented, I prefer another answer: give criticism when the presenter starts preparing for another presentation.

Immediate criticism about how the content was presented can be hard on the presenter's ego. The presenter thinks the presentation was satisfactory, maybe even good or great, and then you come in with bad news. If you give your criticism later, during preparation for the next presentation, you come in with good news: the presenter can be even better, demonstrating improvement just after learning of a problem.

Never show incomplete written work to reviewers

Many cultures offer a variation on the proverb, "Never show work half done to a fool." A corollary is that all reviewers seem like fools when you show them incomplete written work because they cannot help but comment extensively on obvious low-level flaws you already know require work. Such obvious flaws distract reviewers, blocking them from providing the reflective, high-level guidance that you want.

Expect harsh words from anonymous reviewers

Many anonymous reviewers working on behalf of a journal or publisher will be academics who hand such work off to graduate students, who will be eager to show how smart they are by ripping you to pieces no matter how polished your work. Have a thick skin when you receive reviews and be constructive when you review the work of others.

What you need to know

You need to have your speaking and writing critiqued. When you critique, exercise the Golden Rule.

- Never show work half done to a reviewer.
- Ask reviewers where time and energy expended will provide the most improvement.
- Expect harsh words from anonymous reviewers; when you are the anonymous reviewer, be constructive, not gratuitously mean.
- Give advice that is actionable, principled, and positive.
- Offer presentation advice during preparation time.

A good lawyer can keep you out of jail, but no lawyer can get you into heaven.

Robert Watson Winston; American lawyer

Remark to his young son, Patrick Henry Winston

6 Essentials of Ethical Behavior

In this chapter, you learn why you should be ethical for practical reasons. You also learn to defend against communicators who cross the line where persuasion becomes manipulation.

Practice practical ethics

You should behave ethically so as to reflect high values and moral commitment. And I wish, having written that, this chapter would be done, but sometimes values and commitment are not enough, and resolve is best buttressed by practical considerations.

Here is a practical consideration: once you get caught, as an adult, displaying contempt for ethics, you will have destroyed your career. No level of communication skill will help because you will be speaking to or writing for people who do not trust you.

You may not even know your career has been destroyed; associates and superiors may not confront you, but just whisper about you. You wonder why others less capable are advancing, not realizing that it is because your supervisor does not trust you.

Do not plagiarize

One of the classes I teach is discussion oriented and limited to 30 students. I tell them in the first week or so that if a student plagiarizes someone else's work and gets lucky, I will catch them.

Yes, if a cheater gets lucky, I will catch them, yell, give an F on the assigned work, and deposit a sealed letter with the Undergraduate Dean, not to be opened if the cheater stays out of subsequent trouble.

Where is the luck in that? Sometimes the cheater comes to realize that it is easy to get caught and breaks what otherwise might become a lifelong habit.

Where can that habit lead? If you become famous enough, those who do not like you or your ideas will come at everything you say or write with all the power of modern computing. If your thesis, book, or speech has cribbed elements, someone will find them and publish a list showing your cribbed elements juxtaposed with their sources.

Even if what you say or write is only inspired by someone else's work, you subtract nothing from what you say or write by noting that inspiration.

Do not lie, or fib, or even exaggerate

One of my undergraduate advisees drifted into deep academic trouble. He did not seem to have any difficult family issue or health problem, but somehow he could not get himself to attend classes. Alerted by his instructors, I sent messages to him, met with him, listened to his promises to do better, connected him with various sources of help, and hoped for the best. Sadly, when the term ended, he had failed or dropped all but one of four subjects.

At that point, he told me he had faithfully attended classes for a few weeks, then "freaked out." When I spoke to his instructors, hoping to find a forgivable reason, I learned that he had done little homework, missed most examinations, and most importantly, had shown up for classes between zero and three times all semester.

When he told me he faithfully attended classes for a few weeks, that was not a big lie. It was a fib, an unimportant little lie of no consequence. It was no big deal except that I could not tell whether his lying habit was limited to fibs. I had no idea whether he was truthful about important matters of considerable consequence.

Fibbing is an easy habit to develop. Sometimes it is the result of living with a parent inclined to rage if you say the wrong thing. Sometimes it is the result of growing up in a place where you have to lie to stay out of trouble.

When fibbing becomes a habit, it becomes hard to remember which fib you told to whom, increasing the likelihood of getting caught. Keep in mind an aphorism attributed, controversially, to Mark Twain: "If you tell the truth, you don't have to remember anything."

And remember also that once you are seen to lie, fib, or even just exaggerate, you destroy trust. If you are an adult, you may never get it back.

Do not use faked data

You can be wrong about what you expect to do, but you must never lie about what you have done. If you do, you will get caught. If you are at a university and your university is forgiving, you will be allowed to resign; if it is not so forgiving, you will be fired. Either way, your story will be all over the World Wide Web, and as a consequence, you will not get another academic job.

Salute those who have contributed

Sometimes people fail to recognize others in their speaking and writing.

Not only is that unethical, it turns friends into backbiting enemies. When you write, be sure to identify whom you have been enabled by, whom you were inspired by, whose work intersects with what you have done, and with whom you have collaborated. If you are speaking, be especially clear about with whom you have collaborated, and be explicit about who has done what.

For more on acknowledging collaborators, see page 76.

Also, you should indicate the nature of the collaboration. Maybe it was a joint project, broken into independent subprojects:

> My work is part of a joint project. My contribution was to develop and implement a model of M. I worked closely with others who developed and implemented other models. In particular, W developed and implemented a model of X, and Y implemented a model of Z.

At the other end of the spectrum, maybe you and a collaborator cannot remember who contributed what:

> X and I worked on this together. We worked so closely, with so many late-night brainstorming sessions at a blackboard, we agree that it is impossible to tease out which of us did what.

Usually, however, you do remember who contributed what:

> Several of my slides identify by name the collaborators who contributed, in various ways, to the overall success of my work.

45

Mention contrary positions

When there is controversy, you should fairly describe positions that run contrary to yours, citing pros and cons of those positions relative to yours. Let your audience decide if your arguments are persuasive.

Listen to your audience

If you are trying to inform, you have an ethical obligation to know what your listeners know and what they want to know or need to know. Otherwise you waste their time.

If you are trying to sell, you have an ethical obligation to understand what a potential buyer needs. Otherwise you waste their time.

For more on preparing an audience, see page 63.

Accordingly, you need to ask questions and listen to the answers. That may seem obvious, but it is not easy to do when you are preparing an audience because you may not listen to the answers to your questions.

A classic technique for forcing concentration is to repeat back what you think you heard:

> So, as I understand it, you would like me to focus on x.

> Ok, I'll make sure I don't get too technical.

> Well, I know that is a tough problem, but fortunately, I think I can take care of it for you.

Consider ethical implications of your choices

In various places in this book, I include examples involving people I cannot admire in totality. "Can't you find other examples, not involving flawed people?" asked an early reviewer. Unsure about what to do, I brought the matter up with my graduate students, evoking the following views:

- By praising the work, you honor the person. Take out those examples.
- If those are the best examples you know of, you owe it to your readers to include them.
- Take the examples out and you get yourself on a slippery slope that ends with book burning.
- Keep the examples, but call attention to the character flaws; show you disapprove.
- Who are you to throw stones; you must be without sin.
- Keep the examples, but record this discussion in the ethics chapter. Conclude that sometimes there are no easy answers.

That last position carried the day.

Defend yourself against trickery

Some persuasion techniques become unethical because the persuader's goal is to promote a false or unethical idea. Some persuasion techniques always suggest the persuader has crossed the line from telling true stories persuasively to delivering propaganda.

Beware of ideas made intentionally difficult to understand

I was standing next to a colleague listening to an applicant for a junior faculty position. At the end of the talk, I said to my colleague, "What do you think?" He replied, "It must not be very deep; I understood everything."

I suppose it is natural to think that something is deep if you do not understand all of it, and I know some supervisors recommend including something unintelligible in presentations. I consider such inclusions unethical, and when I suspect the technique is being used on me, I find myself somewhere between amused and angry.

Beware of *ad hominem* criticism

Manipulators condemn a person, not just a person's ideas. You know you are in the presence of a manipulator if they say a person is "weak" or a "loser." If a manipulator responds to the slightest criticism that way, the manipulator rises to the level of bully.

Beware of misused authority

Manipulators will often say "everyone knows" to defend an idea that not everyone believes. Sometimes the manipulator will quote a famous person or cite a religious text to defend an idea.

Benjamin Franklin, presumably with a twinkle in his eye, wrote up his own chapter for the book of Genesis, which he would often read to unsuspecting friends. Perhaps the point of the chapter, religious tolerance, justified the means.

Beware of repetition

Manipulators will often repeat, at every opportunity, something they want people to believe. Frequently repeated phrases such as "I categorically deny" often signal guilt. "He says he is innocent" often suggests that whoever he is, he is on thin ice.

Perhaps the most famous repeater was Cato the Elder, a Roman statesman, who is said to have ended every speech with "Carthago delenda est," meaning Carthage must be destroyed. I suppose he could have been advocating repairs to some aqueduct somewhere, and you would still hear "Carthago delenda est" at the end. He got his wish. In 146 BCE, Rome destroyed Carthage completely.

Beware of graphical trickery

For more on being easily deceived, see page 247.

We think with our eyes as well as our words, but our eyes are easily deceived by elegant visuals that deceive accidentally or tricky visuals that deceive deliberately.

What you need to know

- Whenever you speak or write, practice practical ethics: do not plagiarize, lie, or use faked data.
- Mention contrary opinions and treat them fairly.
- Be a good listener, ask questions and repeat back what you think you have heard in the answers.
- Note whom you salute with your examples.

- Whenever you listen or read, defend yourself against trickery: beware of ideas made intentionally difficult, *ad hominem* criticism, misused authority, repetition, and graphical trickery.

- Salute those who have contributed to your work, especially collaborators.

Part II
Presentation

It's easy to play any musical instrument: all you have to do is touch the right key at the right time and the instrument will play itself.

Commonly attributed to Johann Sebastian Bach;
German composer and musician

7 How to Choose Time and Place

In this chapter, you learn the best time and place to make a presentation or provide instruction. You also learn about room shape and room size.

Present in the late morning or midafternoon

Of course, you probably have no choice, but if you do, 11:00 am is a good time to speak. At MIT, just about all students and faculty wake up by then. We all seem to work far into the night, so I do not like to talk before 10:00 am.

I also do not like to talk right after lunch: food makes people sleepy. In the afternoon, 3:00 pm is a good time. Later than that, right before the end of the day, is bad because people want to go home to get started on the second half of the day.

Focus on stories when you speak after dinner

It takes a lot of convincing to get me to speak after dinner because expectations shift from instruction to entertainment after 6:00 pm.

You need to tell interesting stories, preferably laced with humor, to be successful. How much humor? Once I asked a knowledgeable friend, a seasoned after-dinner speaker, for his after-dinner speaking secrets. "About one joke every seven minutes," he said.

Keep your talk short, not more than about 30 minutes, because when the coffee arrives, many will start getting restless, thinking about going home.

Shape matters

At MIT, we have some good lecture halls and some not so good. Huntington Hall, Room 10-250, also known as The Center of the Universe, is my favorite place to lecture.

Huntington Hall, Room 10-250, MIT. Good for delivering talks and lectures. Image courtesy of Gerald Jay Sussman.

The hall is wide, and the seats curve slightly around the speaker. The feeling, for both speaker and audience, is one of surrounding the speaker. Before speaking, the speaker can easily engage with a lot of front-row people.

It has a huge blackboard space with screens off to the side if you want to project a few supporting slides. If you are giving a talk, rather than a lecture, there is a huge screen in the center.

Entry is at the front, but off to the side, partially screened from the speaker. People come and go unobtrusively.

Lighting matters

For more on well-llit rooms, see page 60.

Note that Huntington Hall is well lit. You can go to sleep in there, but you have to be really tired.

Shape can make a good talk bad

Note the contrast with the following hall, which is dark and soporific. It is long and narrow, creating a feeling of separation between the speaker and the audience. Entry is from the rear, so people can come and go unobtrusively, but because entry is from the rear, people tend to sit in the back, far from the speaker, unengaged. There is a big screen, but no blackboards. You can watch a film in here, but it is hard to present and impossible to lecture.

⊘ Good for watching films, bad for presenting lectures.

If you find yourself stuck speaking in such a place, try to welcome early arrivals and encourage them to come to the front. When later arrivals see people in the front, they will tend to go in farther.

Speak in a right-sized place

Of course, you probably have no choice, but if you do, choose a place that will be more than half full. Anything less creates a sense that the smart people are doing something else. You want something like the following.

First day of my class, Introduction to Artificial Intelligence, in Huntington Hall, Room 10-250.

It is even better to have a room where all the seats are taken and a few people have to stand or sit on the floor.

Eventually, my annual *How to Speak* talk overflowed this lecture hall. We moved to Room 10-250 the next year. Image courtesy of Jess Lin, MIT 2012; appeared in *The Tech*, MIT's student newspaper.

If your audience is small, on the order of ten people, the audience will likely sit at a conference table. If you are showing slides, be sure to sit or stand at the screen end, so that people in your audience can see you and the screen without shifting their eyes back and forth as if they were watching a tennis match.

For more on a feel for what it will be like, see page 59.

For more on opening and closing lines, see page 111.

If you are to speak on stage in an auditorium, be sure to get a feel for what it will be like to speak on the stage before the audience arrives. Practice your opening and closing lines; work your way through some or all of the rest of your talk; move around and get comfortable. Otherwise, being on a stage is likely to cause stage fright.

What you need to know

Time and place help determine your presentation success.

- The best time to present is late morning or midafternoon.
- The best room shape is wide, rather than narrow, with a surrounding feel.
- The best lighting is full up and bright; use natural light from windows if possible.
- Avoid rooms entered from the rear; people will sit in the back, making it harder to engage.
- The best room size is such that it will be at least half full. Overflowing is good because that makes it clear that something important is happening.
- When speaking at a conference table, be sure to sit or stand at the screen end.
- When speaking on a stage, be sure to get a feel for what it will be like before you start.

The place where Harris had been encamped a few days before was still there and the marks of a recent encampment were plainly visible, but the troops were gone. My heart resumed its place. It occurred to me at once that Harris had been as much afraid of me as I had been of him. This was a view of the question I had never taken before; but it was one I never forgot afterwards. From that event to the close of the war, I never experienced trepidation upon confronting an enemy, though I always felt more or less anxiety. I never forgot that he had as much reason to fear my forces as I had his. The lesson was valuable.

Ulysses S. Grant; American Civil War general and 18th President

From the *Personal Memoirs of Ulysses S. Grant* (1885)
1994 edition published by Smithmark Publishers Inc., page 149

8 How to Prepare the Ground

In this chapter, you learn that on the day of your presentation, you need to do some preparation so as to avoid avoidable problems. You learn, for example, about dealing with the lights, preparing yourself, and preparing your audience.

Prepare the place

Whenever I go somewhere to speak, the first thing I ask my host is to show me where I will be speaking. I want to get a feel of what it will be like to speak there. If there are surprises, I want to know about them long before I am scheduled to start talking.

Decide where you will stand

Generally, you should avoid a lectern and plan to move around a bit, calmly, as you speak. If you are being recorded, and audiovisual technicians insist on immobilizing you, be sure you stand or sit close to your visuals.

For more on avoiding lecterns, see page 113.

Speak to a virtual audience

On my visit to the place where I will speak, I imagine saying my first few sentences to a virtual audience. Sometimes I imagine an audience composed of disinterested, noisy farm animals. That way, no matter what the audience turns out to be like, I know it cannot be that bad.

Ensure water is handy

Sometimes I dry out when I speak; I do not know why. I always make sure there is some water handy for those occasions when xerostomia emerges unexpectedly. I use water because when I spill it on myself, it dries without a stain. If you think you might find it awkward to drink something during your talk, practice taking a drink from time to time while you speak to a virtual audience.

Prepare for audio-visual disasters

It was horrible. I thought my slides were ready, but somehow my laptop and their AV system hated each other. Somehow my slides advanced on their own and could not be stopped. After several restarts, the audio-visual technician asked, "Should we try again?" I replied, "Not in this life," and somehow just talked my way through an abbreviated version of what I had to say.

Each time something like that happens, I add one more thing to my disaster list so as to be ready if it ever happens again. Here are some examples:

- There is no wireless microphone. Insist on a wireless microphone in advance. You do not want to be trapped behind a lectern.
- There is no adapter to connect your laptop to their AV system. Bring your own set of adapters.
- Your laptop crashes. Bring a copy of your talk on a thumb drive.
- Your embedded videos do not run. Be ready with a verbal description.
- The remote control does not work. Have the audio-visual technician advance your slides. Do not say, "Next slide, please." Agree with the technician on a subtle next-slide-please gesture instead.
- The audio-visual equipment does not work at all. Bring hardcopies of your slides and use them as an outline for an extemporaneous, slide-free talk.

Get the lights full up

During final preparation, I determine who might adjust the lights. If it is a lecture hall with a big audience, there probably will be an audio-visual specialist. "Keep the lights full up," I instruct.

"Oh, but your slides will look better if we dim the lights."

"Maybe," I reply. "But slides are really hard to see through closed eyelids."

Many of my talks are to university audiences, which guarantees everyone is tired. Dimming the lights, especially after a meal, signals to the human body that it is time to go to sleep. Bright lights signal sunrise. Time to wake up.

Of course, this means you should construct slides that are easily appreciated in a fully lit room. Eschew pastel colors; use black text on a white or light background.

The mechanisms that enable us humans to tell, understand, and recombine stories separate our intelligence from that of other primates.	The mechanisms that enable us humans to tell, understand, and recombine stories separate our intelligence from that of other primates.

⊘ Pastel colors wash out. If you use them, you will have to dim the lights. Everyone will go to sleep. Use black text.

Similarly, do not use white text on a black or dark background:

The mechanisms that enable us humans to tell, understand, and recombine stories separate our intelligence from that of other primates.	The mechanisms that enable us humans to tell, understand, and recombine stories separate our intelligence from that of other primates.

⊘ Black or other dark background color invites dimming the lights. Everyone will go sleep. Use a white or light background.

Prepare yourself

Whenever I go to an athletic event, I am struck by how much the athletes stretch as they prepare. They know there are things you just have to do to be ready to perform at the highest level. Likewise, when you speak, there are things you just have to do.

Be a little nervous

Being nervous is a natural consequence of any fight-or-flight situation. You are going to fight and win because a little nervous energy comes out as enthusiasm and passion. Because you need to be a little nervous, there is no point worrying about it. Just develop and practice the ground-preparing rituals described in this chapter. Those rituals will keep your adrenaline at the right level.

Take a walk

If you are much more than a little nervous, then take a quick walk around the block just before you speak. The walk will calm you down. Breathe deeply.

Psych up

If I have done a presentation many times, I may not be nervous enough; I worry about being flat.

If circumstances are right, as in a big lecture hall, I fire up the sound system and play a song, often one by the Rolling Stones or will.i.am and the Black Eyed Peas. The music gets my adrenalin flowing and wakes up the students.

If playing something on the sound system fails a too-quirky test, then I use inconspicuous ear buds.

By way of a safety net, I just play something in my head. *Ode to Joy*, the fourth movement of Beethoven's Ninth Symphony, works well for me.

Warm up

You have to enunciate distinctly. No amount of electronic amplification can compensate for talking with your mouth almost closed or your vocal chords unprepared.

Just as athletes warm up their muscles before contests, actors and musicians warm up their voices before performing. You should, too.

You can try the sorts of phrases and tongue twisters musicians use, such as these samples from vocalist David Gordon:

The lips, the teeth, the tip of the tongue,
the tip of the tongue, the teeth, the lips.

A box of biscuits,
A box of mixed biscuits,
And a biscuit mixer. (Gordon, 2016)

Personally, I prefer to go outside and bark like a dog. I try to be
sure no one is within earshot, but occasionally someone in the
vicinity, unaware that I am warming up, thinks me odd. If you
worry about this sort of thing, try coughing in various ways or
pretend to be clearing your throat instead of barking.

Compose and memorize your opening sentences

When you start your talk with a few carefully composed and memorized sentences, you know you will get off to a good start; you
know that the words will keep flowing.

For more on memorized openings, see page 111.

Prepare your audience

You do better if you sense your audience is with you. You do worse
if not. You need to do what you can to ensure that your listeners
start out with a positive attitude.

Chat with the early arrivals

I get to the place where I will speak quite early so I can chat with
those who get there early, too. "Hi, I'm Patrick Winston," is usually enough to get a conversation going. Then, I generally get to,
"Is there anything you would especially like me to talk about?"

By the time you get around to a few people, you will have some
friends in the audience. They make you feel more comfortable,
they will have a positive attitude, and that positive attitude can be
infectious.

Once I asked my colleague Gerald Jay Sussman why a large class
seems to click some years and not others. "It's strange," I said.
"You would think with 300 or 400 students, the law of averages

would dictate that each year would feel the same, but that's not the way it works."

"It's symmetry breaking," he said, calling to mind a deep idea from physics that, fortunately, has a simple analog in spinning coins. The stable states of a coin are lying down showing heads or tails, but while the coin is spinning, the situation is symmetric, and you cannot tell which state the coin will be in when it falls over.

Sussman added, "The students don't realize it, but they all want to be like everyone else, so on the first day of class, they are all sensing the overall mood. Within a few minutes, the symmetry breaks spontaneously, and the class falls into a fixed state."

I asked, "So, if you don't do well in the first few minutes of the first day, you've had it, and there is nothing you can do after that?" "Yes," he replied.

Knowing the importance of those first few minutes, Sussman has his teaching assistants sit down in front during his first lecture. They are instructed to nod approvingly and frequently, and laugh at all the jokes.

Gerald Jay Sussman always has happy teaching assistants sit in the front row for the first lecture of the semester. Image courtesy of Gerald Jay Sussman.

You probably will not be able to bring any sort of entourage to do the work of those teaching assistants, but the people you get friendly with before your talk are conditioned to do the nodding and laughing.

Establish eye contact

Just before you deliver your first sentences, you should establish eye contact with a few of your new friends. A second or two each is enough. It gives them a warm feeling. As your presentation progresses, focus on those who appear enthusiastic, not those who seem angry, critical, or bored.

What you need to know

Before your talk, work your way through a checklist to ensure that you are ready to go. Include at least the following in your warm-up ritual:

- Look over the place where you will speak early on.
- Make sure you have water handy.
- Make sure all the audio-visual equipment works.
- Get the lights full up, and make sure they stay up.
- Know that being nervous is good. Take a walk, breathing deeply, to keep your adrenalin under control.
- Psych up with power music, possibly played only in your head.
- Exercise your voice.
- Chat with the early arrivals.
- Establish eye contact with happy listeners.

Where you can learn more

Scott Berkum tells you a lot about preparing the ground, and what can go wrong, in *Confessions of a Public Speaker* (Berkum, 2010). Berkum is engaging, funny, and highly informative.

The beginning is the most important part of any work....

Plato; Greek philosopher

From *The Republic*, written about 380 BCE,
(Plato, 2016), page 260

9 How to Start

In this chapter, you learn how to start a persuasion talk, with special emphasis on slide-based talks. Many such talks are given as part of a job-interview process. Small differences can determine whether you get the attention of busy people and that will determine whether you get the job or someone else with lesser ideas but better communication skills gets the job.

Be glad to be there

Because we humans are social animals, people go to talks even if they could get the same content from an on-line recorded talk or something written down. We like to feel we are part of an event. We like to see what others think and tell them what we think.

Audiences especially like to think that the speaker is glad to be there, that the speaker wants to talk to them, and that the speaker has prepared something at least a little special for them.

When Steve Jobs introduced the iPhone during his keynote address at MacWorld 2007, his first words were, "This is a day I've been looking forward to for two-and-a-half years" (Thomas, 9 January 2007). No doubt about it, he was glad to be there.

Maybe you are not introducing a big product, but there is sure to be some honest reason why you are glad to be there.

You could say, "I'm honored to be here," but I do not recommend it. It is trite, and if you are honored to be there, everyone already knows it. If it is not much of an honor, it will look like a gratuitous fib you always start with.

Somehow, when someone says they are honored to be somewhere, I think of rock concerts I've been to where the star says, "Hello Boston!" or something like that. It never feels very genuine. I imagine that the star just asked the stage manager, "Where did you say we are tonight?"

Instead, talk about how eager you are to talk about something they are interested in and you are passionate about. Or, you can talk about how great it is to shed some light on what should be done. Or, you can talk about how great it is to be back in your hometown with all the fond memories that evokes.

Something will come to mind if you put a little effort into thinking why you really are glad to be there; if you cannot think of anything, you should have declined to speak.

Express your *Vision*

Because you have to convince your audience that you have a Vision, you should start with a slide titled *Vision*.

What is your Vision? There are two parts:

- You are focused on a big problem that a lot of people care about or think interesting.
- You have an idea about how to solve it.

The following example illustrates.

Explain your Vision. The problem is to understand human intelligence. The idea is to model human story-processing.

Vision
If we are to develop a computational account of human intelligence, then we have to understand our human ability to create, tell, and understand stories.

The slide illustrates the *if-then* way of expressing a Vision. The problem is in the *if* part; the approach, in the *then* part.

In *What to Put at the Beginning* (page 177), you learn that the *if-then* opening is just one of several ways of expressing your Vision. Here are some more:

- The interesting-story opening.
- The big-questions opening.
- The mission-blocker opening.
- The new-opportunity opening.
- The imagine-what-it-would-be-like opening.

Explain your *Steps*

Once your Vision is clear, your next step, presenting your *Steps* slide, demonstrates that you have a plan and that you have done something already.

<table>
<tr><td colspan="2" align="center">Steps</td></tr>
<tr><td colspan="2"></td></tr>
<tr><td>•</td><td>Specify behavior</td></tr>
<tr><td>•</td><td>Formulate computational problems</td></tr>
<tr><td>•</td><td>Collect appropriate representations</td></tr>
<tr><td>•</td><td>Implement a system</td></tr>
<tr><td>•</td><td>Perform experiments</td></tr>
<tr><td>•</td><td>Crystallize principles</td></tr>
</table>

Explain the Steps you are taking toward realizing your Vision.

You do not have to have completed all the steps. You can show the whole plan and announce where you are, "Here are the steps in my plan. I'm working on step four; I'm implementing a system."

Thrill with *News*

Right up front, tell everyone what you have just been able to do or are just about to do. Such News tells your audience that they have the privilege of seeing something fresh and new; you are not telling them about something you did a decade ago. It is new and exciting and you could not tell them about it if you had come a day or week or month earlier.

Use right-now words such as the following when explaining the News.

Just *yesterday*, my system...
For the first time, in *February*...
Tomorrow, we will turn this on and...

Avoid using the word *recently*; *recently* can mean recent relative to when the Egyptian pyramids were built.

Using the following slide pair, for example, I might say:

I focus today on summarization of the sort a system can do only if it understands a story. I explain how my Genesis story-understanding system discovers a Pyrrhic victory in this 80-sentence outline of the plot of *Macbeth* and compresses the outline into a six-sentence summary. The summary shown here reflects improvements I made just this past week.

Two slides convey
the News.

News	News
Macbeth is a thane and Macduff is a thane. Lady Macbeth is evil and greedy. Duncan is the king, and Macbeth is Duncan's successor. Duncan is an enemy of Cawdor. Macduff is an enemy of Cawdor. Duncan is Macduff's friend. Macbeth defeated Cawdor. Duncan becomes happy because Macbeth defeated Cawdor. The witches danced and had visions. Macbeth talks with the witches. The witches predicted that Macbeth will become king. The witches astonish Macbeth. Duncan executes Cawdor. Macbeth becomes Thane of Cawdor. Duncan rewarded Macbeth because Duncan became happy. Macbeth wants to become king because Lady Macbeth persuaded Macbeth to want to become the king. Macbeth invites Duncan to dinner. Duncan complements Macbeth. Duncan goes to bed. Duncan's guards become drunk and sleep. In order to murder Duncan, Macbeth murders the guards and Macbeth stabs Duncan. Macbeth becomes king. Malcolm and Donalbain flee. Macbeth's murdering Duncan leads to Macduff's fleeing to England. In order to flee to England, Macduff rides to the coast and Macduff sails on a ship. Then, Macduff's fleeing to England leads to Macbeth's murdering Lady Macduff. Macbeth hallucinates at a dinner. Lady Macbeth says he hallucinates often. Everyone leaves because Lady Macbeth tells everyone to leave. Macbeth's murdering Duncan leads to Lady Macbeth's becoming distraught. Lady Macbeth has bad dreams. Lady Macbeth thinks she has blood on her hands. Lady Macbeth kills herself. Birnam Wood is a forest. Burnham Wood goes to Dunsinane. Macduff's army attacks Dunsinane. Macduff curses Macbeth. Macbeth refuses to surrender. Macduff kills Macbeth.	The story is about Pyrrhic victory. Macbeth wanted to become king because Lady Macbeth persuaded Macbeth to want to become king. Macbeth murdered Duncan, probably because Duncan was a king and Macbeth was Duncan's successor. Macduff fled to England. Macbeth killed Lady Macduff. Macduff killed Macbeth, probably because Macbeth angered Macduff.

For more on the
too-many-words
crime, see page 82.

I include the first of the two slides only because I want to show the size and character of what the system analyzes. I suggest reading a sentence or two. Then, I pause briefly to let everyone in the audience do that, move on to the second slide, and pause again to let everyone read the content of the second, which takes about 10 seconds. Without the pauses, I would have committed the too-many-words crime.

If you have just developed a robot that walks naturally, a video is News. Marc Raibert, founder of Boston Dynamics, uses exciting News videos all the time.

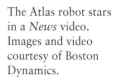

The Atlas robot stars in a *News* video. Images and video courtesy of Boston Dynamics.

Video available via QR code:

What you need to know

Whenever you deliver a persuasion-oriented talk, be sure you get off to a great start by preparing your audience and by including essential elements within the first five minutes.

- Explain why you are glad to be there.
- Explain your Vision: identify the problem and announce your approach.
- Express your Vision as an if-then statement or in one of several standard forms.
- Explain your Steps, demonstrating that you have a plan.
- Thrill with News, making everything you talk about current.

Saying "Thank you" at the conclusion of a talk may not be fatal, but it is often an opportunity-squandering blunder.

Patrick Henry Winston; American computer scientist, professor, and writer

10 How to Stop

In this chapter, you learn how to conclude a persuasion presentation. You learn that most presenters squander their concluding slide with standard, but useless, words.

Conclude with *Contributions*

You do not want the title of your final slide to be *Conclusions*. Conclusions are thoughts that you have, not what you have accomplished. Also, Conclusions carries a sense of finality, suggesting there is nothing more to be done, discussed, followed up, or find exciting.

In a slide-based talk on research, your final slide will be visible longer than any other slide, so it occupies a valuable position. If you answer questions or a discussion starts or you are the final speaker before a break, your final slide could be up on the screen for 20 minutes. You have no alternative: the title must be *Contributions*.

When you title your final slide *Contributions*, it tells everyone you have made Contributions.

```
┌─────────────────────────────────────────────┐
│  ┌─────────────────────────────────────────┐ │
│  │             Contributions               │ │
│  └─────────────────────────────────────────┘ │
│                                               │
│   •  Developed model of human story-processing │
│   •  Introduced six kinds of inference reflexes│
│   •  Performed three Genesis-system            │
│      experiments: story retelling, summarizing,│
│      and authoring                             │
│   •  Speculated about self-awareness           │
│                                               │
└─────────────────────────────────────────────┘
```

The only proper title for the last slide in a slide-based research talk.

Note that the order of elements in the *Contributions* slide helps shape any following questions or discussion. A final element starting with *Speculated...* invites discussion, and if a lively discussion does follow, it will help people remember you and what you have said.

Use active verbs in your *Contributions* slide

Note that all the elements in the example use active verbs. They come from the following list of especially appropriate verbs. Note that each verb suggests a concrete Contribution:

analyzed	described	enabled	formulated	proposed
argued	designed	enumerated	hypothesized	proved
articulated	determined	established	identified	showed
created	developed	exhibited	implemented	speculated
demonstrated	discovered	explained	introduced	suggested

Avoid *improved* and all its synonyms; *improved* suggests incremental work of little importance.

Contributions come in many forms

Just about every kind of persuasion talk should end with a recital of Contributions, but *Contributions* is not the right title for every purpose. Here are alternatives to consider:

- For a study-group report, conclude with a slide titled *Recommendations*.

For more on business briefings, see page 301.

- For a business-briefing talk, conclude with a slide titled *Business messages*.
- For a sales presentation, conclude with a slide titled *Assured benefits*.

For more on concluding a business plan, see page 185.

- For a new-venture pitch to venture capitalists, conclude with a slide titled *Projected earnings*.
- For a donation request, conclude with a slide titled *What your gift will do*.

For more on ending political speeches, see page 78.

- For a political speech, you are not likely to show slides.

Do not squander opportunity

There are many ways to squander your opportunity to assure your audience that you have actually done important work.

Say no to Thank you

The following is the worst possible, but frequently seen, final slide, the *Thank you!* slide.

Thank you!

⊘ Do not use this slide. It squanders opportunity.

Thanking the audience is a weak move. It subliminally suggests to listeners that they have done you a favor by showing up for a talk by a speaker who lacks self-confidence. Because your talk was wonderful, the audience should be thanking you.

For more on weak move, see page 77.

Do not end with an equally weak final slide, the *Questions?* slide.

Questions?

⊘ Do not use this slide. It squanders opportunity.

If there are questions, such a slide will be up on the screen for 20 minutes occupying space that should be used to remind everyone about the contributions that you have made.

Another way to squander opportunity is to show a slide with a URL. I have seen thousands of people witness such a slide, but I have never seen anyone copy down the URL.

⊘ Do not use this slide. It squanders opportunity.

> More at:
>
> http://people.csail.mit.edu/phw/index.html

But wait. What about recognizing your collaborators on the final slide? You should recognize your collaborators, and they will be, legitimately, extremely upset if you do not, but you need not recognize them in the final slide.

⊘ Do not use this slide. It squanders opportunity.

> Collaborators:
>
> Winston Churchill, Patrick Henry, Martin Luther King, Abraham Lincoln, and others

Recognize your collaborators up front, on the title slide of your talk.

Acknowledge collaborators up front, not on a final slide.

> *How to Speak*
>
> Patrick Henry Winston
>
> in collaboration with
>
> Winston Churchill, Patrick Henry, Martin Luther King, Abraham Lincoln, and others

If you recognize collaborators on a final slide, not only do you squander the opportunity to call attention to your Contributions, but you also deliver the wrong message. A natural reaction is, "Hmmm. Nice piece of work, but not such a big deal when you divide by 4+."

I emphasize that you must be sure to be explicit, throughout your talk, about what you have done personally, what you have done jointly, and what you have benefited from that you did not do yourself. It is the right thing to do; your collaborators will develop strong antibodies against you if they think you are claiming credit for their work.

For more on acknowledging collaborators, see page 45.

What about just announcing you are done as follows? These might be good concluding slides if your talk actually includes no Contributions, so you have nothing to put in a *Contributions* slide and no reason for your audience to listen to you.

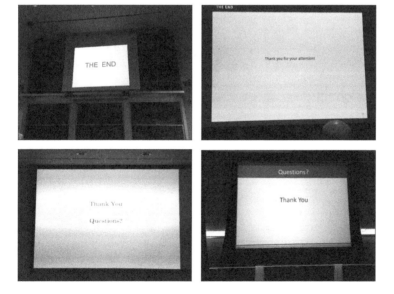

⊘ No comment.

Say yes to a salute

How do people know it is time to clap? Your talk, after all, is not an orchestral performance; if it were, you would walk over to the concertmaster and shake hands.

You could say, "Thank you." Or worse yet, really horrible, you could say, "Thank you for listening." Like a thank-you slide, both signal that you do not think you were worth listening to, and suggest that the people who stuck it out for your entire talk need to be thanked for a difficult-to-endure courtesy.

The impression you want to leave with your audience is that it was a privilege to hear you speak, not torture.

Saying "Thank you" is not fatal, but it is a weak move, especially if there is a skeptic out there in the audience looking for a sign of insecurity.

Instead, you can say, "And now, my presentation is over, and I am ready for questions." That is fine, but it just puts off the inevitable need to tell the audience it is really over.

President Bill Clinton, in his 2012 Democratic Party Convention speech, finished his talk with a classic benediction: "God bless you, and God bless the United States of America."

President Clinton finishes speech. In the video, you can see him press his lips together, as if suppressing the thank-you instinct, just before he concludes with a salute.

Video available via QR code:

Of course, if you are giving, say, a job-interview talk at MIT, it would be odd to say "God bless you, and God bless the Massachusetts Institute of Technology." Instead you can use the basic contributions closing: "And now, with this summary slide listing what I have contributed, my talk is concluded." Then, you walk over and shake hands with your host. Everyone will know it is time to clap.

And if they do clap, it is acceptable to nod or mouth a silent "thank you" because at this point you are acknowledging the applause.

Or, after you have reviewed your Contributions, you can use a joke closing or story closing. Then, shake hands.

For more on closing with a joke, see page 154.

Or, better still, you can use the verbal salute closing: Here is how I conclude my annual *How to Speak* talk at MIT:

For more on closing with a story, see page 153.

> So, there you have it. You know more about speaking than you knew an hour ago, maybe a lot more. By coming, you acknowledge the importance of knowing how to communicate, and I salute you for that. Make sure your friends come next year.

And then I walk over to someone I know and shake hands.

What you need to know

- Your final slide should be titled *Contributions*; such a slide highly influences what people in your audience think about your presentation.

- You squander your opportunity to display your Contributions when you end with a slide carrying nothing but *Thank you!*, or *Questions?*, or a list of collaborators, or a URL.

- Do not thank your audience to conclude your talks; instead, end with a reference to your Contributions, a joke, a story, or a salute.

*Your work is ingenious. It's quality work. And there are
simply too many notes, that's all.*

Joseph II, Holy Roman Emperor

Remark to Wolfgang Amadeus Mozart in the film *Amadeus*,
directed by Milos Forman for Orion Pictures, 1984

11 How to Compose Slides

In this chapter, you learn to keep slides simple. In particular, you learn to minimize the number of words you put on a presentation slide and what happens if your slides contain too many words. You also learn about reveal-slide alternatives, blackout slides, rabbit holes, and progress bars.

Slides are a blessing, slides are a curse

Technical persuasion talks generally involve slides because in a persuasion talk, you are exposing ideas at high speed, not instructing. People in your audience will not be taking an examination, after all, so they need to follow what you do, but they do not need to be able to reproduce what you do.

Also, in science, engineering, business, architecture, medicine, and many other fields, you need slides to show off pictures, tables, graphs, and mathematics. Maybe you need to show a picture of your nanotechnology apparatus, a collection of neurons, or an archaeological dig. Maybe you need to talk about a mortality table, a projected earnings spreadsheet, or the inflation rate over the past decade. Maybe you want to explain, in summary form, the kind of mathematics that led you to develop a new learning algorithm.

All that is reasonable. What is not reasonable is to subject an audience to a document outline on a screen, with bullet lists, often deeply nested, on slide after slide. That kind of slide show amounts to a presentation Golgotha.

Edward Tufte, in his eloquent philippic against Microsoft Power-Point and other slideware, tells us that the problem lies in word count. You cannot get enough words on a slide, he says, to convey a complete, true statement. His solution is to get rid of your slides (Tufte, 2006).

Another solution is to use a smaller font so as to get more words on a slide. That approach does not work because people cannot read and listen to you at the same time. The more words you lay down, the less you are heard.

Use simple slides with a minimal number of words

I had just landed at Logan, Boston's airport, after returning from a conference. It was a rough flight; I felt like I was riding inside an unbalanced washing machine. I decided to have a cup of coffee at an airport cafe before heading home.

Just as I sat down, trying to relax, someone walked up to me and asked, "Are you Professor Winston?"

"I think so," I replied, trying to be funny.

He explained that he was on his way to give an interview talk in Europe, and that he had seen a video recording of my *How to Speak* talk. He asked, "Would you mind critiquing my slides?"

"Not at all," I said, "You have too many slides, and they all have too many words."

He looked puzzled. "How do you know?"

"It is always true."

Then, we went through his slides, noted that there were too many slides and too many words, and discussed how and where to prune. A week or so later, I learned he got the job offer.

If he had found me in my office instead of the airport, I would have asked him, as I generally do, to print out his slides and lay them out on a table. Often the result looks like this.

⊘ Too many words. The talk is dense and needs air. The slides are blurred so as not to embarrass the author.

The following slides are better. Many slides have no words; others have few words; those with many words are not meant to be read.

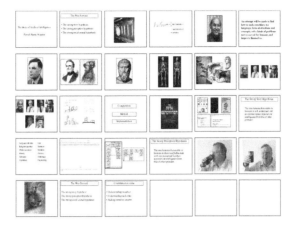

Not so many words.

We have only one language processor

There is good evidence that we humans have only one language processor and that it is easily jammed (Hermer-Vazquez et al., 1999). If you jam a listener's language faculty by piling too many words on a slide, the listener has nothing left with which to listen.

High-pressure salespeople know this, so they never stop talking, limiting your ability to think. Students who text, read email, or surf the web during lectures know this because they do not get anything out of the lectures they attend.

One of my students, Mitchell Kates, did a term project in which he ran a pilot study to determine how people deploy their language processors when listening to a talk. He constructed a presentation about Django, a web tool, which he gave to two groups of volunteers, also known as freshmen in his fraternity. One group received 50% of the information on the slides and the other 50% orally; for the other group, the information on the slides became oral information and the previously oral information was written on the slides.

Sample slide from language-processor experiment. Image courtesy of Mitchell Kates.

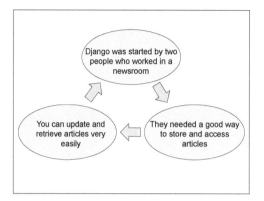

Interestingly, both groups did 75% better when answering questions about the information on the slides rather than about the information given orally. In subsequent discussion, one of the subjects said, "I wish you hadn't talked so much. It was distracting." If you have a lot of words on your slides, as in the experiment, people read them and do not listen to you. You might as well just send someone in to click through your slides silently while you find something else to do.

Slash, shorten, shrink, trim, and cut

If you use a slide such as the following, you should expect no one to listen to you or come to hear you speak again.

⊘ This slide has serious problems. Get rid of the background. Theme and clip art from Microsoft PowerPoint.

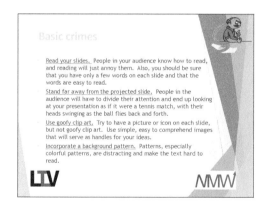

The first problem is the background pattern, often called a theme. Do not use such background patterns; they are distracting.

Basic crimes

- Read your slides. People in your audience know how to read, and reading will just annoy them. Also, you should be sure that you have only a few words on each slidewords are easy to read and that the words are easy to read.

- Stand far away from the projected slide. People in the audience will have to divide their attention and end up looking at your presentation as if it were a tennis match, thith their heads swinging as the ball flies back and forth.

- Use goofy clip art. Try to have a picture or icon on each slide, but not goofy clip art. Use simple, easy to comprehend images that will serve as handles for your ideas.

- Incorporate a background pattern. Patterns, especially colorful patterns, are distracting and make the text hard to read.

LTV   MMW

⊘ Get rid of the clip art and logos. Clip art from Microsoft PowerPoint.

Next, get rid of the goofy clip art. Some people think clip art makes a slide look better and more interesting. It does not.

And while you are at it, you do not need your organization's logo on every slide. If you can, get rid of it, except, perhaps, on your title slide.

Note, however, that organizational policy may require ubiquitous use of logos, and your organization may require a copyright notice on each slide, partly for legal reasons, especially if viewers are likely to ask for copies. You may be able to keep everyone happy by putting logos and notices only on hardcopy handouts and electronic distributions, keeping the slides you present detritus free.

Basic crimes

- Read your slides. People in your audience know how to read, and reading will just annoy them. Also, you should be sure that you have only a few words on each slidewords are easy to read and that the words are easy to read.

- Stand far away from the projected slide. People in the audience will have to divide their attention and end up looking at your presentation as if it were a tennis match, thith their heads swinging as the ball flies back and forth.

- Use goofy clip art. Try to have a picture or icon on each slide, but not goofy clip art. Use simple, easy to comprehend images that will serve as handles for your ideas.

- Incorporate a background pattern. Patterns, especially colorful patterns, are distracting and make the text hard to read.

⊘ Too many words. Prune.

Now, the conspicuous problem is too many words. The temptation for you to read out loud to your audience is overwhelming, but reading out loud annoys many and enrages some.

Once I attended a meeting of a NASA advisory committee charged with providing advice about robots in space. Carl Sagan, a pioneering astronomer, chaired and sat at the head of a large U-shaped table. Marvin Minsky, a founder of the field of Artificial Intelligence, sat nearby.

About halfway into the day, Minsky interrupted a speaker and asked him to stop reading his slides. The speaker fell apart. Reading had been such a crutch, he soon went back to reading. Minsky, noted for kindness toward students, had little patience for adults he thought should know better. He walked out.

Get rid of the words and leave the ideas. If you put all those words into your speaker's notes, you have what you need to say out loud. Otherwise, you might as well just flip through your slides silently.

⊘ Simplify the title.

Basic crimes

- Read your slides
- Stand far away from the screen
- Use clip art
- Use a background pattern

In light of the *simple-is-better* principle, that red box has got to go.

Better.

> **Basic crimes**
>
> • Read your slides
>
> • Stand far away from the screen
>
> • Use clip art
>
> • Use a background pattern

You may even decide to get rid of the title entirely. Thinking carefully about a title forces you to think about the role a slide is to play. But once thinking about a title has served that purpose, you may not want to keep it. After all, you are going to introduce the topic orally: "Now, I want to tell you to avoid basic crimes committed by well-intentioned but undereducated speakers."

No title. You explain what the slide is about as you speak.

> • Do not read
>
> • Stand close
>
> • Delete clip art
>
> • Eliminate background patterns

Annotate review copies

I never distribute slides to people for use when I am presenting. While distributing slides simplifies note-taking, it also becomes a distraction to everyone when impatient listeners start flipping through their copies.

Sometimes, I do distribute annotated copies of my slides for use before or after a presentation.

Before presenting, if someone proposes to hire me to give a talk to a commercial audience, I send a copy of the slides I propose to use, annotated with slide titles and supplementary captions, to ensure they really want to hear what I will say.

For more on slides left behind, see page 303.

After presenting, I may also supply annotated copies of the slides I have presented. Sometimes I leave behind annotated slides because people in the audience are expected to write a summary for someone not attending. Sometimes people in the audience are evaluating my work for a sponsor and want access to what I have said as they write a report. Sometimes people in the audience want to reflect on recommendations I have made on behalf of a study group.

I always include not just titles and captions but also clarifying words in leave-behind recommendation slides, knowing that recommendation slides are likely to be quoted and possibly attacked.

Use more words on your slides if you are not a native speaker

If your speech is hard to understand, you should have a few more words here and there on your slides to ensure that your Vision–Steps–News· · · Contributions story and your key ideas are readily understood. I write this with trepidation; do not think it is a license to show slides such as the *Basic Crimes* slide on page 85.

Solve the look-ahead problem

I confess I use slides with bullet lists, but I agree with Nancy Duarte, who points out that the people to whom you are presenting always read ahead, so they are bound to be looking at the final bullet while you are explaining the first one (Duarte, 2008).

One alternative is to transform your ordinary list into a *reveal* list, so called because with each click, a new line is revealed.

• Do not read	• Do not read • Stand close

⊘ Replace the list with a reveal list. Each new line appears as you talk about it.

• Do not read • Stand close • Delete clip art	• Do not read • Stand close • Delete clip art • Eliminate background patterns

Note, however, that reveal lists are known to drive many people crazy. Some of those driven crazy are more accepting of a *highlighted list*, so called because only one line, the one you are talking about, is highlighted; the rest are dimmed.

• **Do not read** • Stand close • Delete clip art • Eliminate background patterns	• Do not read • **Stand close** • Delete clip art • Eliminate background patterns

Replace the reveal list with a highlighted list. Use dimmed type for all lines except the one you are talking about.

• Do not read • Stand close • **Delete clip art** • Eliminate background patterns	• Do not read • Stand close • Delete clip art • **Eliminate background patterns**

Even highlighted lists, if many, become tiresome. Spreading the list out, one item per slide, is another possibility.

Let each slide announce what you are talking about, when you are talking about it.

Do not read	Stand close
Delete clip art	Eliminate background patterns

Some designers would complain that spreading out the list leaves each slide with too much white space. Fortunately, once you have spread a list out, you have plenty of room to incorporate a reinforcing graphic. You may even eliminate the words entirely.

In the following, I show how I get rid of the bullet list in the sample reveal slide. With the first slide, I explain that you should reduce word count. As a joke, I read a few lines of the text. With the second slide, I ask where the speaker is, noting he is missing in action, not close to the slide, so the slide, not the speaker, becomes the focus. With the third slide, I discourage clip art. With the final slide, I rail against distracting background themes.

⊘ Too many words. Speaker out of sight. Goofy clip art. Distracting theme. Clip art and theme from Microsoft PowerPoint.

Use bullet lists sparingly

Many presentations consist almost entirely of bullet lists in some form. Such presentations tend to be maximally boring and unintelligible.

Avoid the temptation. Use bullet lists sparingly, so that when you do use a bullet list, you can draw attention to, for example, steps in a plan, what the listener is to do, or Contributions.

For more on uses of bullet lists, see page 165.

Which method is best for displaying lists is controversial, but keep in mind that any approach becomes tiresome if used too often. Ten reveal slides in a row are noted by all and resented by many. Use two or three in your presentation, if you must, but think hard about how you can get rid of them.

For more on displaying lists, see page 3.

Show how the elements fit together

Bullet lists not only bore, their habitual use encourages a rigid way of thinking, much like traditional outlining methods. Whenever you have a bullet list, you should ask yourself if there is a graphic way to show how the bullet elements fit together.

For more on traditional outlining methods, see page 29.

In my Artificial Intelligence research, I make a big fuss about what I believe to be the distinguishing characteristic of human intelligence. Here is a summary:

> Robert Berwick and Noam Chomsky argue that we humans, and only we humans, have the neural mechanism needed for symbolic thought (Berwick and Chomsky, 2016). With what they call *merge*, we build deeply nested symbolic descriptions of relations and events. Convincing evidence indicates that chimpanzees, with DNA almost identical to ours, do not have merge; there is no persuasive evidence the Neanderthals had it either.
>
> I believe merge matters to science because the merge idea provides a foundation for research aimed at shedding light on how we humans understand, tell, and creatively compose stories about people and things, and on how those capabilities enable much, perhaps most, perhaps all, of education. The merge-enabled story faculty enables us humans to exhibit cultural bias, retell for instruction, retell for persuasion, tie new situations to old, summarize, negotiate, reason, follow recipes, self-program, be self-aware, and perform many other cognitive human capabilities.

I could cram that story into a bullet list for a slide.

⊘ A fascinating story, told in a boring way.

- Other animals perceive and remember sequences
- We alone have *merge*
- Merge supports story processing
- Story processing enables recipe processing
- Recipe processing enables reasoning and self-programming

I do not use that slide. Instead, I note that *merge* is like the keystone in an arch, working together with other capabilities in the rest of the arch to enable story understanding. The keystone metaphor emphasizes that, while there is only a small change, there is enormous enablement.

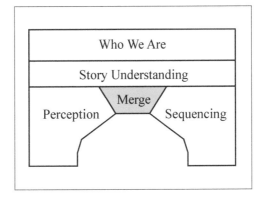

A fascinating story, told in a way that highlights how *merge* is like the keystone in an arch, enabling story understanding and uniquely human thinking.

Use blackout slides

Suppose you mostly want to speak, but there are a few images you want to show to add drama to your talk. You should put *blackout slides*, slides that are completely black, in between those you want to show. Otherwise, much of the time you will be showing a slide unrelated to what you are saying.

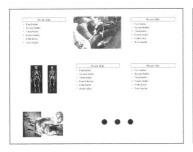 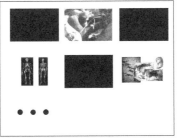

Blackout slides interdigitated with pictures. Slides are condiments, not the pièce de résistance.

Your remote control, with which you advance your slides, may have a blackout button, which, when pressed, makes the screen go black. Blackout slides have an advantage: if you lose your remote

For more on prearranged, unobtrusive hand gesture, see page 113.

control, nothing really bad happens. You will just have to arrange for a friend to advance your slides when you make a prearranged, unobtrusive hand gesture.

For more on dimming the lights, see page 60.

Note that blackout slides would leave everyone in the dark if someone has dimmed the lights, but you should not let anyone dim the lights anyway.

Eliminate animated transitions

You can have entire slides or parts of slides fade in, fly in, float in, bounce in, or worse. Do not do that. Animated transitions distract, like background patterns.

Consider a progress bar

I often find myself wondering if a speaker will ever stop.

On such occasions, I feel much better if I have a visual sense that the speaker is progressing and the end will come. If your talk has any prospect of seeming like one of those talks that never end, put in a progress bar.

Slide with blue progress bar. The length of the bar increases as the talk progresses. Evidently, the speaker is about done.

Can a machine be self-aware?

Another approach, less elegant, is a page counter.

Can a machine be
self-aware?

30/32

Slide with slide
number. Evidently
the speaker is about
done; he is on slide
30 of 32.

You should not use the page-counter approach if you have too
many slides; if your first slide has 1/200 in the corner, no one will
even pretend to pay attention.

For more on having
too many slides, see
page 82.

Use large fonts

Make yourself a test slide.

This is 25-point Times

This is 30-point Times

This is 35-point Times

This is 40-point Times

This is 50-point Times

This is 60-point Times

This is 72-point Times

Times font sizes in a
Microsoft
PowerPoint slide.

Project your test slide where you will be speaking. Look at it from
where someone seated far away would see it.

A test slide as seen by
a distant viewer.

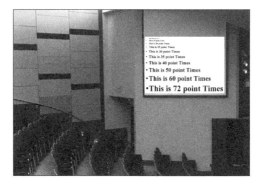

You will probably decide that you should have a good reason to
use anything smaller than a 40-point font and an extremely good
reason to use anything smaller than a 35-point font. Bigger is better, in part, because bigger helps ensure you avoid the too-many-
words problem.

For more on
too-many-words
problem, see page 82.

Alternatively, suppose you know that your slides will be projected
on a screen of known width and that people in the back row will
be a known distance from the screen. Print the test slide on a standard size sheet of paper. Look at the printed test slide and pick a
minimum font size that you can easily read. Then, you should
avoid using a font smaller than the one given by the following
formula:

$$\text{Font size} = \frac{\text{Width of test paper}}{\text{Width of screen}} \times \frac{\text{Viewer distance}}{\text{Test distance}} \times \text{Test font size}$$

Generally, large rooms come with large screens, so you are not
likely to need the formula. Just use 40-point fonts or bigger and
know that a font smaller than 35 points cannot be read easily.

Note that when printed on paper, the top of the 72-point T should
be about one inch, or 2.54 centimeters, above the bottom of the
72-point p. Of course, when displayed in a computer screen the
difference may be bigger or smaller, and when projected on a
screen the difference will be a lot bigger.

A *type family*, such as Times and Helvetica, is a set of related
typefaces, such as regular, italic, and bold. A *font* is a typeface in
a particular size.

In *How to Select Type Families* (page 235), you learn that a serif type family features characters that have supplemental lines at the ends of the strokes. A sans serif type family has no such lines.

For more on serif type family, see page 236.

I prefer serif type families for slides, and I insist on serif type families for books (except for section headers), because I find serif type families more readable, but I acknowledge that type-family selection is controversial and hotly debated.

Include pictures of involved people

Many business presentations show stock photographs of unfamiliar, but happy people, or worse, cute baby animals. That seems pointless and silly to me, especially when the same images seem to pop up in unrelated talks. On the other hand, when talking about ideas, it is interesting to see pictures of the people who conceived the ideas. For example, when I talk about what sorts of research projects make sense, I often refer to remarks like these that caution against following the herd.

Marvin Minsky:
If everyone is doing it, don't.

John Laird:
If it would get done anyway,
do something else.

The advice of Marvin Minsky (image courtesy of Juliana Minsky) and John Laird (image courtesy of John Laird) on what problems to work on. Pictures of the quoted give life to the slide.

Use the right number of slides

How many slides should you include in a technical talk? How much time should you spend talking about a slide? Of course, it all depends on how much you pack into each of them. If your slides are denser than they should be, plan on spending three minutes or so on each slide; if they are airy, as they should be, maybe you will spend one or two minutes on each slide. You should expect to talk for about 30 minutes if you have prepared 20 slides.

Include rabbit holes

No matter how much time you allocate per slide, you will have too many slides. Just about everyone fears that there will not be enough material to fill the allocated time, so they load up their slide sets with too many slides. Then, they either sprint toward the end or awkwardly flip past slides, annoying many people.

The solution is what I call a *rabbit-hole* slide, after *Alice's Adventures in Wonderland* (Carroll, 2017). Think which slides you can eliminate when you inevitably come up short on time. On the slide just before those you can eliminate, put in a hyperlink, which, when clicked, skips over the slides you want to skip.

In the following slide of a painting by Karen Prendergast, the hyperlink is attached to the big yellow rectangle on the lower right.

A rabbit hole showing hyperlink area. Image courtesy of Karen Prendergast.

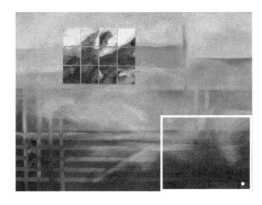

When you click in the vicinity of the yellow dot, you skip over the optional slides. Of course, I get rid of the yellow border of the hyperlink rectangle and just leave the yellow dot; it reminds me that I have a rabbit hole.

A rabbit hole indicated by unobtrusive yellow dot. Image courtesy of Karen Prendergast.

Honor community expectations

Now, with the right number of simple slides and some judiciously placed rabbit-hole slides, you are ready to go.

Actually, if your subject requires no visual support, you could go further and just talk. Many people have, after all, seen enough slides for a lifetime.

Nevertheless, you have to be sensitive to people in your audience and what they expect, need, and want. A misstep renders people bored or hostile.

At technical conferences, slides supply detail, usually too much

Slides aimed at technical audiences tend to be too many, too wordy, and too complicated. Some have to be complicated, and some have to have mathematics, but you should still keep it simple. I drew the following from my slide collection. Note that I rarely use titles.

The messages spoken with these slides are: (upper left) you learn more if you explain the material to yourself (image courtesy of Michelene Chi); (upper right) revenge occurs when harm leads to harm in the other direction; (lower left) now mice can be made to have photoelectric neurons (image courtesy of Ed Boyden); (lower right) the dawn of AI appeared with a program that did symbolic integration like an MIT undergraduate student.

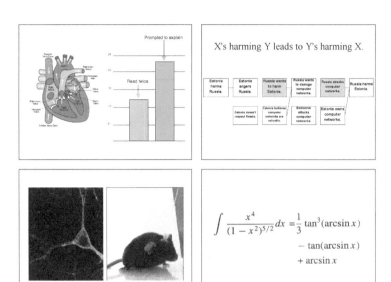

At business-leadership meetings, slides iconify concepts

Slides aimed at business-leadership audiences tend to have few words, no titles, lots of pictures, and professional design. Here are a few examples adapted from slides seen in a few minutes of web browsing:

The messages spoken with these business-leadership slides would be: (left) keep it simple; (right) the AI economy is exploding.

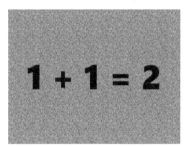 

The messages spoken with these business-leadership slides would be: (left) today's business world is awash in many kinds of data; (right) your customer has gone digital; have you?

Community expectations vary

You readily see the contrast between the slides on the left, prepared for a technical audience, versus slides on the right, that carry the same points to a business-leadership audience.

Images replace words. Title removed, as said by presenter.

Exciting Times!

- IBM's Watson
- iRobot's Roomba
- Google's Firefly self-driving car
- Boston Dynamics's Atlas robot
- Apple's Siri

The Third Wave

A group of young people playing a game of frisbee

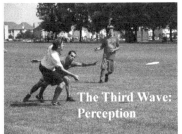

The Third Wave: Perception

Image expands to fill slide. Title embedded in picture. Caption, generated by a deep neural net, is removed, as said by presenter. From Vinyals et al. (2014). Image courtesy of Oriol Vinyals.

Quotation embedded in picture of person quoted. Title removed, as said by presenter. Image of Marvin Minsky speaking at Dartmouth College in the mid-sixties courtesy of the Minsky family. Quotation from Brad Darrach's article in *Life Magazine*, 20 November 1970.

For more on business-leadership slides, see page 100.

> Minsky's Scary Prediction
>
> Once the computers get control, we might never get it back. We would survive at their sufferance. If we're lucky, they might keep us as pets.

After dinner, stick with pictures

If you are doing a travelogue, or otherwise need to show slides in an after-dinner talk, stick with pictures and get rid of the words. Follow the guidelines suggested in the discussion of slides for business-leadership meetings.

For political speeches, just talk

Many claim that visuals are more memorable than words, yet politicians rarely use slides. There are several reasons; here are some:

- Politicians want to be the focus. They do not want you looking at a screen; the screen is not the candidate.
- They deliver many speeches in stadiums, parking lots, or other places where slides are impracticable.
- They talk to TV viewers. Slides would not be seen at all or only with awkward flipping back and forth from face to slide.
- They know there are many ways for a slide show to derail. The projector may not work or be of poor quality. The screen may be too small. Getting everything connected may cause an awkward delay.
- They fear that material on a slide can be caricatured. They know it is harder to retreat from a picture or something written rather than from a misworded phrase.
- They need to keep track of what is happening on a teleprompter. Looking at a slide makes it easy to lose track.

- They know that looking back at a slide prevents engagement.

- They do not want to be conspicuously untraditional.

President Ronald Reagan used no slides when he spoke about East-West relations at the Brandenburg Gate in West Berlin (Reagan, 1987). He did, however, use the large prop behind him to great advantage.

For more on props, see page 107.

A really engaging speaker just speaks. Here President Reagan, the Great Communicator, commands, "Mr. Gorbachev, open this gate! Mr. Gorbachev, tear down this wall!" Image courtesy of Ronald Reagan Library.

Of course, President Reagan could have used a slide aimed at a business-leadership meeting.

Few words, no titles, a picture, and professional design. Suited to some audiences, perhaps. Image courtesy of Ronald Reagan Library.

President Reagan could have even used a slide with a nice design and some bullet points of the kind you see too often at conferences.

⊘ Many words, a title, distracting background theme (from Microsoft PowerPoint). Not suited to any audience.

For more on human props, see page 110.

President Reagan was fond of using human props. In contrast to slides, human props are both effective and reliable.

What you need to know

If you are giving a slide-based presentation, be sure to adhere to the following principles:

- Use simple slides containing a minimal number of words.
- Annotate review slides, especially recommendation slides.
- Use bullet lists sparingly.
- Arrange slide elements so they show how your ideas fit together.
- Use blackout slides when you mostly talk and need only occasional visual support.
- Include a progress bar so your audience will know you are making progress.
- Use large, easily read fonts.
- Include pictures of relevant people.
- Expect each slide to consume one to three minutes.
- Use rabbit-hole slides to ensure you finish on time.
- Use slides of the kind that meet audience expectations: concepts for business-leadership meetings; details for technical conferences; and none for political speeches.

Also, do not annoy your audience in any of the standard ways:

- Avoid background patterns, clip art, and stock images.
- Do not overload slides with text; use large fonts to avoid temptation.
- Do not use reveal slides; avoid excessive use of bullet lists.
- Do not read the text on your slides.
- Do not use animated transitions.

You learn more about type in *How to Select Type Families* (page 235). You learn more about using pictures in slide-based presentations in *How to Work with Images* (page 251).

Where you can learn more

For good examples of slide sets prepared by graphic designers for business-leadership meetings, see Nancy Duarte's book titled *slide:ology* (Duarte, 2008) and Garr Reynolds's book titled *presentationzen* (Reynolds, 2012).

Bob, that boy's going to MIT!

James Horner Winston; American lawyer

Remark to his son, Robert Watson Winston, on returning home to find his young grandson, Patrick Henry Winston, pointing at a large hole in the roof of the family garage, the result of a failed effort to turn lead into gold

12 How to Use Props

In this chapter, you learn that one or two physical props make your oral presentations memorable. You also learn about using human props.

Great communicators use props

I learned about props from A. R. Gurney, a noted playwright, who happened to be one of my undergraduate humanities instructors at MIT. He explained that he and other playwrights think hard about the objects actors handle on stage, the props.

To emphasize the importance of props, Gurney had us study *Hedda Gabler*, Henrik Ibsen's play about an unhappy, hard-to-please woman, a somewhat boring husband, and the husband's rival for an academic position. As the play opens, there is a pot-belly stove, faintly glowing with embers. The rival has just finished a magnificent manuscript, which ensures he will get the position the husband wants. The embers in the stove become brighter. The rival, drunk, loses the manuscript, which Hedda somehow acquires. The stove's fire is roaring now. You just know that the priceless manuscript, conspicuous in Hedda's hands, will find its way into the stove, and it does.

I have forgotten much of what happened in the play, but I have never forgotten the stove and the manuscript. Somehow, as Gurney noted, audiences pay attention to physical objects.

Props aid memory

In my annual talk on how to speak, I rail against the use of pointers. To emphasize my dislike, I break a wooden one into pieces. Years later, people mention that they remember what I said about pointers especially.

Do not use a pointer. Breaking one drives the idea home.

Sometimes I mention that my mobile phone has 50,000 times more power and memory than the computers people considered amazing when I was a graduate student. Naturally, I exhibit my mobile phone; it has become a prop.

A mobile phone used as a prop; 50,000 times more power than any computer at the dawn of Artificial Intelligence.

Even if your prop is too small for anyone to see, the prop can still be effective: "I have in my hand the world's smallest robot, smaller than a housefly."

Props add emphasis

Props work, and not just in plays. Once, while I was staying at a ranch in Montana with my wife and my daughter, the county sheriff strode into the dining room where we were eating dinner to announce that a forest fire was approaching rapidly. "You don't have to leave," he said, "but if you choose to stay, I have here a

Sharpie." He held it up and paused for dramatic effect. "I want you to use it to write your name and social security number on your belly so we can identify your body later." We got the message and left immediately. The Sharpie prop did the trick.

Physical props dominate pictures

Do not replace physical props with slides that have pictures. Using a prop is better because a prop adds emphasis and aids memory.

The priceless manuscript and the roaring fire. Image courtesy of Karen Prendergast.

Props prevent monotony

Many presentations become monotonous because they consist of a seemingly endless sequence of slides. To defeat that kind of monotony, introduce a prop.

Using a spinning bicycle wheel to demonstrate conservation of angular momentum beats a dry lecture any day. Image courtesy of Paul Keel.

The Great Communicator used human props

Props even make political speeches memorable. President Ronald Reagan started the tradition of using people as props in his State of the Union addresses. He pointed out various people in the gallery, noting, in particular, how Lenny Skutnik's heroism saved the life of a drowning flight attendant when Air Florida Flight 90 crashed into the Potomac River in Washington, DC, in 1982 (Frantzich, 2011).

Lenny Skutnik, used as a human prop. Video courtesy of Ronald Reagan Library.

Video available via QR code:

What you need to know

Playwrights use props because props add drama and establish focus. You can, too:

- Props add emphasis.
- Props help prevent monotony.
- Physical props are more memorable than a picture of the same object.
- Carefully selected props make talks truly memorable.

13 Adopt Good Habits

In this chapter, you learn characteristics of great speakers that you should incorporate into your own speaking. You also learn vitality-destroying habits of weak speakers that you must avoid.

Choreograph your opening and closing lines

You want to start off strong and finish strong, so you should work hard to open and close your slide presentations with a few well-thought-out lines.

Accordingly, you should memorize a few opening sentences. In those sentences, you can explain why you are glad to be there (but not honored to be there), and you can start to articulate your Vision, both of which you need to do to attract your audience's attention in the first minute or two.

For more on glad to be there, see page 67.

For more on honored to be there, see page 67.

You should also memorize a few closing sentences just as you memorize a few opening sentences. That way, you avoid the weak, thank-you move.

For more on thank-you move, see page 77.

Note that you should not write out and memorize your entire talk. It will sound like written language, losing the extemporaneous feel you want. If you should have a memory failure, you will panic and want to curl up into a little ball. Use memorized lines only to get yourself off to a good start and to finish with polish.

There are exceptions. If you are delivering a very short talk of 15 minutes or less, you may feel more confident if you write out and memorize your talk so as to eliminate redundant elements and awkward attempts to speed up.

If you are a politician, you probably read speeches written for delivery using a teleprompter. You get away with it because your speech writers know how to write language that does not sound written. Because each sentence is studied by your opposition, eager for ammunition, having your speech written out and studied in advance helps you avoid a lot of trouble.

Winston Churchill, interestingly, was his own speech writer. It is said that, because he had a slight speech impediment, he wrote out and read his speeches, in part, so as to avoid words that begin or end with the letter *s*.

Unless you have a good speech writer, or a speech impediment, or you are speaking in a language in which you lack fluency, you should not read when you present.

Divide your talk into enumerated parts

Many listeners have short attention spans, some say as short as six minutes. You can do such listeners a favor by dividing your talk into parts with a kind of oral punctuation. You just say, "My talk has three parts. The first part is about how we got here ...." Then, later, "And now, we have come to the second part ...."

Oral punctuation tells people who have fogged out when they can start listening again.

If you want to emphasize your part changes, you can buttress your oral markers with transitioning slides.

These four transitioning slides broke a 40-minute talk on Artificial Intelligence into five parts of six to ten minutes each.

How we got here:
The beginning

Where we are:
Current excitement

What we can do next:
From perception to cognition

What's next after next:
Aspects of self-awareness

Avoid the lectern

Lecterns always seem to turn up where meetings happen. I do not know why. Beware. Lecterns turn perfectly normal people into motionless zombies.

Some nervous speakers pace back and forth, annoyingly, but most hide behind lecterns. Some grip them as if in fear of falling over. Good speakers move around and gesture, calmly, as they speak.

Do not hide behind a lectern. Use it to support a glass of water or your notes or your laptop.

Insist on a wireless microphone if the room is large; be unwilling to be stuck at a lectern because the only microphone available is attached to it.

Use a remote control

Without a remote control, you are tethered to your computer, and you have to return to it with every transition to a new slide. Alternatively, you stand hunched over a lectern or table. Either way, you have to look down awkwardly to find the right key, which punctuates your talk in a kind of staccato unrelated to what you are saying.

Suppose you forgot to bring your remote. No worries. Ask a friend to be your remote control, pressing the advance key on your computer on seeing a unobtrusive, prearranged gesture from you, such as raising a finger.

Decline the laser pointer

Once, while we were watching a presentation, one of my students turned to me and whispered, "We could all leave, and he wouldn't know!" All we could see was the back of the speaker's head because he constantly sprayed his slides with a laser beam. It is a wonder those beams do not drive audiences into epileptic fits.

It really is obvious. When you use a laser pointer, you have to look back at the screen to aim it. When you do, you show, at best, the side of your head to the audience, and more likely, the back of your head, as in the following whimsical image of me pointing at my head in an image in which I am pointing at my head recursively.

⊘ Laser pointer, a bad idea.

For more on point, see page 119.

But what if you really do have to identify something in your slide? If the room is small, you can get into the projection and point. If the room is large, embed an arrow, maybe a lot of them, numbered, in your slide.

Embedded arrow, a good idea.

Some presenters can use a laser pointer with taste, but most cannot. If you have a laser pointer that is part of a remote control, and you want to use the buttons to move from slide to slide, cover the laser with a bit of tape so you won't be tempted to use it.

Laser pointer modification; an engineering solution to a pernicious problem.

What about using an ordinary pointer instead? I do not recommend them. Everyone who uses them cannot seem to avoid waving them around. And, if you are close enough to use one, you probably are close enough to point with your hand.

For more on ordinary pointer, see page 107.

For more on point with your hand, see page 119.

Get a display between you and the audience

Laser pointers force you to look back at the screen but even without a laser pointer, the screen will draw you like honey draws bears because you have to look back at it to be sure which slide is displayed.

You will not have to look back if you are in an audio-visual nirvana. With top-of-the-line audio-visual arrangements, a big display is in front of you, between you and the audience, so you do not have to look back to see what is on the screen in back of you.

With a large display showing you what is on the screen behind you, you need not look back. Here, another display shows the time.

You can improvise. Use the lectern or a chair to hold your laptop.

Improvised display. With this, you do not have to look back at the screen behind you.

Note that the wire connecting the computer to the display is taped to the floor. Even if you are confident you will not trip on a loose wire, people in your audience will be distracted if they perceive a tripping hazard. Professional production groups generally include a chief electrician, also known as the *gaffer*, who ensures that wires running across the floor are taped down with, what else, *gaffer's tape*.

Do not play with your hair

If you have a beard, keep your hands off it; if you have long hair, keep your hands out of it. Stroking a beard and wrapping hair around a finger signal nervousness.

When you play with your beard or hair, you might as well hold up a sign saying, "I'm nervous."

Keep your hands out of your pockets

If you put your hands in your pockets, everyone will know you are nervous. People who ordinarily never put their hands into their pockets put them into their pockets when they speak. It is as if they had never seen their hands before and do not know what to do with them; it is as if their hands were private body parts that should be kept covered up in public.

When you put your hands in your pockets, you might as well hold up a sign saying, "I'm nervous."

If not in your pockets, where can you put your hands? I once visited a convent church in Serbia. Thinking I was being respectful, I clasped my hands behind my back. A nun came up quickly and pulled them apart. In her culture, like in many, hands have to be visible to show you are not concealing a weapon.

Thus, putting your hands either in your pockets or behind your back is a bad idea. What, then, do you do with them?

You can point.

I much admired Seymour Papert's lectures. As I tried to figure out what made his lectures so engaging, I went to one and focused on technique rather than content. I noted that Papert pointed a lot at the blackboard. And then, amazed, I noted that he frequently pointed at places that had nothing to do with what he was currently talking about!

Papert pointing at the blackboard to emphasize an especially important idea. Image of Papert from a 1968 lecture courtesy of Gerald Jay Sussman.

Or, you can clasp your hands together in front of you, especially if you are seated at a table.

Or, you can make magnificent gestures. Steve Jobs, when he introduced the iPhone during his keynote address at MacWorld 2007, used one when he spoke about the iPod precedent:

Jobs talking about Apple history at MacWorld 2007.

Video available via QR code:

Point with care

Note that people raised in some cultures consider it rude to point at anything with your index finger. Generally, you will be on safe ground if you point with an open hand, but even that may offend.

If you point with your index finger, you may be unintentionally rude in some parts of the world, so you should learn to point with an open hand.

Check with someone knowledgeable of local norms when you speak in unfamiliar places.

Wear the right clothes

Wear clothes in which you feel comfortable. If you never wear a tie or if you never wear high heels, do not wear them during your presentation. If you do, you will feel as awkward as you would if you were wearing a clown suit, and it will show.

Of the clothes in which you feel comfortable, wear clothes that honor community expectations, and that usually means clothes at the upper end of what you wear every day. If you show up in clothes that do not honor community expectations, everyone will remember what you wore, not what you said, and you will fail.

Finally, check yourself out in a mirror, front and back, to be sure you look the way you want to look.

Maintain eye contact

The eyes of great presenters do not drift away from the people to whom they are talking. Great presenters do not stare at the ceiling, empty chairs, pillars, or walls, none of which can appreciate what they say.

Some great presenters pick out a few people they know, scattered throughout the audience, and cycle their eyes from one to the next.

Others use the W method: you start by moving your eyes to the left rear of the audience, then to the front a quarter of the way to the right, and eventually trace out a W.

The W pattern. You move your eyes this way periodically to ensure eye contact.

And, of course, great presenters are not so busy aiming a laser pointer that they cannot keep their eyes on the audience.

Eliminate fillers and grunts

It was really horrible. The auditorium was packed. The topic was fascinating. The presentation was polished. The speaker was being honored in a way that comes along once in a lifetime.

Then, I noted the *uh* fillers. They came so fast I counted, in one five-minute interval, on average, one *uh* every five seconds. The speaker had no idea the *uh*s were there; many in the audience did.

For more on critiquing your talk, see page 39.

What should you do? You may well not note your own use of a filler. People who you ask to critique your talk may not note the fillers or may not want to hurt your feelings by telling you that they are there. Your only recourse is to make a list of instructions for those who critique your talk and include the specific instruction, "Watch for filler words, such as *uh*, *ah*, and *um*, and stop me if I use any."

Avoid up talking

Some English speakers have a habit of ending declarative sentences with a rising pitch, making the sentences sound like questions. Try saying, "Many think the habit suggests insecurity," with *insecurity* spoken at a higher pitch. You will sound insecure. Then, try saying, "Many find the habit irritating," with *irritating* spoken at a higher pitch. You will, perhaps, irritate yourself.

Mind the time

When you drone on too long, you lose your audience. They leave in spirit if not in body.

If there is a visible clock, watch it. Do not use a wrist watch; looking at it a lot will make people think you have a flight to catch.

If there is no visible clock, use a friend. Have your friend sit in the back and then stand when you have, say, 10 minutes left. Then it will be time to get aggressive in your use of rabbit holes. Arrange other signals with your friend—crossed arms and the like—to signal when you really should stop.

For more on rabbit holes, see page 98.

Stick to one or two central themes

Once I gave my *How to Speak* talk to biologists at Boston University. Afterward, one of the faculty members came up to me and said, "The trouble with most faculty candidates is that they think they have to tell us about everything they have ever done, so they end up telling us nothing."

But you really do want people to know you have done a lot of successful work. So, you say, "Over the past few years I've done x, proved y, and demonstrated z. Today, I want to focus on my latest result and current focus, showing how you can turn lead into gold using ordinary chemicals found in everyone's kitchen," or something along those lines.

Be positive

If you say you are unprepared, you invite resentment. If you say you are nervous, you encourage people to feel sorry for you, rather than listen to you. If you say you are unaccustomed to public speaking, you make obvious what most of the people in your audience might otherwise fail to note. If you keep apologizing for an audio-visual failure or for speaking in a language that is not your mother tongue, you merely draw attention to the problem, making it worse.

For more on the too-many-words crime, see page 86.

If your speech is difficult to understand, then you are excused from the too-many-words crime; you can write out on your slides the most essential points of your talk.

Be ready for a flat audience

What if you are excited but your audience is not? What if you tell a joke and no one laughs? What do you do if you feel like you are at the bottom of the Grand Canyon speaking to stones?

First, know that you are not alone. It happens, and usually for reasons that have nothing to do with you. Second, try to make a joke about it. The comedian Milton Berle said this: "What is this, an audience or an oil painting?"

Think about how to answer questions

When you are asked a question, you have no time to reason about how to respond; you have to react. Accordingly, you need to know about some standard ways to react.

Repeat each question

Repeat each question you are asked because most of the audience will not have heard it. No one likes listening to an answer without knowing to what question the answer is directed.

Also, when you repeat the question, you help ensure you understood the question.

Failing to remember to repeat each question is easy. I ask someone in the front row to signal when I forget.

Be self-confident when asked a question you cannot answer

Sometimes someone asks a question for which you do not have a good answer. Never try to bluff. Do not apologize. Just say, "That is a great question" (all questions are great), then execute one of the following maneuvers:

The confession maneuver

- That question hasn't occurred to me before, so I'll have to think about it.
- I don't have an answer right now, but I'll get back to you.

Do not use the confession maneuver too often. When Facebook CEO Mark Zuckerberg testified about privacy and the use of customer data before the US Senate Judiciary and Commerce Committees in 2018, more than 20 of his answers were variants of "I'll have my team get back to you on that." Much was made of his overuse of that kind of answer.

The after-the-talk maneuver

- I don't have an easy answer for that; let's discuss it after my talk is over.
- I don't have a brief answer to that; let's discuss it after my talk is over.

If you see that there are a lot of questioners queued up, you might say that is why you want to deal with questions that deserve long answers later.

The not-yet maneuver

- I don't know the answer, but that question deserves a lot of thought.
- I've been thinking about that, but I haven't reached a conclusion yet.

The hard-problem maneuver

- Answering that question is way beyond where we are today.
- Answering that question will take years.
- That question deserves more thought than it is getting.
- I hope more people will work on answering that question.

Be ready for hostile questions

Some questioners make comments, disguised as questions, to show how smart they are.

In my talks on story understanding, I sometimes use a 100-sentence summary of Shakespeare's *Macbeth* to illustrate how the Genesis story-understanding system sees regicide, revenge, and Pyrrhic victory in the summary even though none of those words or their synonyms appear in the 100 sentences.

A hostile person in the audience once started going on at length about how *Macbeth* could not be understood without reference to the political realities of Elizabethan England. Somehow he felt compelled to show everyone that he knew a lot about Shakespeare. What he actually showed was that he missed the point of the example.

For more on after-the-talk maneuver, see page 123.

Usually, I respond to such comments with the after-the-talk maneuver or one of the following:

The thank-you maneuver

- Thank you for your comment. I find it thought provoking.

If the questioner gets my blood up, I may choose a more aggressive response, especially if I am sure everyone else in the audience is with me:

The with-all-due-respect maneuver

- With all due respect, I think your question is a bit off point.

This is a hostile answer you should use only if you want to be seen to fight back, not deflect. When you say "With all due respect," you imply that the amount of respect due is zero. When you say "a bit off point," you imply completely off point.

The what's-wrong-with-you maneuver

- I'm not sure if you intend that as a comment or an insult, but in either case let's be civil and discuss it in private.

Be ready for no questions

Some audiences have no questions. Maybe your talk was clear beyond description. Maybe nothing was clear and no one can think where to start. More likely, the audience is just tired.

But there you are; you have announced it is question time, and no one asks a question. To deal with such situations, having a few questions to ask yourself works well. You need only say, "Well, while you are reflecting, let me ask myself a question I think important." If there are no questions forthcoming after one or two of those, you can declare question time over and move on to a terminal salute.

For more on terminal salute, see page 77.

Imitate great speakers

Whenever I see and listen to a good lecture, talk, or speech, I ask myself why it is good, then if it is recorded, I look again, because we humans are great imitators. Once I articulate to myself what features make something good, and then focus on those features as I witness good speaking, I find myself adapting various kinds of features naturally into my own speaking.

For more on great imitators, see page 198.

From good speakers, I have absorbed ideas for opening and closing, VSN-C delivery, slide composition, use of props, overall structure, gestures, eye contact, and ways of expressing passion. Without watching good speakers and asking *why*, I could not have written much about how to speak.

For more on VSN-C, see page 8.
For more on passion, see page 157.

On the other side, I learned to avoid speaking tethered to a lectern, showing too many slides with too many words, waving a laser pointer, letting hands drift into pockets, using filler words, and up talking. Without watching poor speakers and asking *why*, I could not have written much about bad habits.

Compose stirring phrases

Great speakers deliver their truly big ideas with those ideas dressed in the finest clothes. Once you listen to or read what they have said, you may well find yourself adapting what they have said to new needs with new phrasings. The following are some of my favorites.

In 1775, Patrick Henry demanded immediate action as the Revolutionary War commenced:

> Our brethren are already in the field! Why stand we here idle? (Copeland and Lamm, 1973)

Winston Churchill exhorted the people of Great Britain to resist what appeared to be certain defeat by Nazi Germany early in World War II:

> Let us therefore brace ourselves to our duties, and so bear ourselves that, if the British Empire and its Commonwealth last for a thousand years, men will still say, "This was their finest hour." (Churchill, 1940)

For more on slogan, see page 15.

The speech became known as Churchill's *Their finest hour* speech. The stirring phrase became a kind of slogan.

Stirring phrases often include alliteration, a series of closely connected words that begin with the same sounds. President John F. Kennedy used alliteration in expressing the commitment of the United States to liberty:

> Let every nation know, whether it wishes us well or ill, that we shall pay any price, bear any burden, meet any hardship, support any friend, oppose any foe to assure the survival and the success of liberty. (Kennedy, 1961)

What you need to know

- Choreograph your opening and closing.
- Divide your talk into enumerated parts.
- Do not let a lectern imprison you.
- Use a remote control, but not a laser pointer.
- Do not look at your slides. Get a display between you and your audience.
- Get loose wires taped down to avoid tripping.
- Do not play with your beard; do not play with your hair.
- Keep your hands out of your pockets.
- Point with an open hand, not your index finger.
- Wear the right clothes; be comfortable and honor community expectations.
- Maintain eye contact.
- Eliminate fillers and grunts.
- Avoid ending declarative sentences with a rising pitch.
- Finish when you are supposed to finish.
- Stick to one or two central themes.
- Never demean yourself.
- Always repeat questions asked from the audience.
- Practice standard maneuvers for answering questions you cannot answer.
- Have answers to hostile questions and be ready for no questions.
- Learn good habits by studying great speakers, asking *why*.
- Compose stirring lines to convey big ideas.
- Stirring lines often become identifying slogans.

Part III

Instruction

Plan your work for today and everyday, then work your plan.

Commonly attributed to Margaret Thatcher; British stateswoman, politician, and Prime Minister

14 How to Prepare to Instruct

In this chapter, you learn how to prepare to instruct, with attention to broadly applicable essentials and the special demands of traditional lectures.

Instruction and communication intersect

In the pre-digital world, especially in the humanities, students read, came to class to discuss, and wrote papers. In the pre-digital world, especially in science and engineering, students attended lectures, did homework and problem sets, and took examinations.

Now, in the digital world, there are other ways, including the flipped class and the totally online class. When a class is flipped, students watch online lectures, delivered in 10-minute chunks interdigitated with short quizzes. Students go to class to discuss, to debate, to do experiments, to solve problems, or to work together in groups. When instruction is totally online, online discussion groups replace classes.

What is the right way to instruct in light of all that is newly enabled? Some instructors demand technology on the cutting edge; others stick with blackboards and chalk. Some students prefer live lectures; others sleep through them and want instruction online. Overall, the right way seems to depend on the instructor, the student, the subject, and what is to be learned.

No matter what you decide is the right way for your situation, your choice will benefit from broadly applicable communication essentials. Those essentials are what this chapter is about.

Attend to broadly applicable essentials

Many steps are the same whether you prepare for discussions, lectures, flipped classrooms, or online instruction. They are the same whether you are instructing in a university or delivering corporate training.

Identify learning outcomes

I once spoke with a colleague about using slides in the classroom. "You use quite a lot of slides," I said. He replied, "Yes, that way I can cover more material."

I thought to myself, "You need to think not only about what you want to cover in your lectures, but also about what you want your students to be able to do." That is, you want to identify desired outcomes.

Noted educator Benjamin Bloom chaired a committee that developed a taxonomy of learning outcomes way back in 1956 (Bloom et al., 1956). Now slightly revised, Bloom's taxonomy consists of six levels acquired from bottom to top (Anderson and Krathwohl, 2001).

Revised Bloom's taxonomy.

Many instructors put a lot of time into detailed outcome descriptions, using Bloom's taxonomy, arguing that such effort helps them allocate time and plan examinations. Bloom's taxonomy invites critique, however. Some argue that the level distinctions are vague; others argue that the top three layers in the taxonomy describe competences that should be acquired simultaneously, not sequentially from the bottom.

Revised Bloom's taxonomy, redrawn to emphasize that several competences are acquired simultaneously.

Analyze	Evaluate	Create
Apply		
Understand		
Remember		

Accordingly, while you should think about learning outcomes, you may decide to develop your own, simpler approach to taxonomy. You may, for example, choose to think mostly about the *Apply* and *Evaluate* elements, with the expectation that the *Remember*, *Understand*, and *Analyze* elements emerge automatically as by-products.

Whatever taxonomy you use to help you allocate time and design examinations, note that no taxonomy helps you know how to structure an engaging hour of instruction. For that, you need to read *How to Deliver a Lecture* (page 143). Also, Bloom's taxonomy does not help you to be inspiring. For that, you need to read *How to Inspire* (page 157).

Empowerment promises create interest

The beginning and end of a class are the most important parts. You need to start with a carefully crafted empowerment promise and conclude by noting that you have delivered on your promise.

Usually, your promise will implicitly correspond to one of Bloom's levels. In a lecture on games, you might promise your students that they will understand how the Deep Blue chess-playing program worked (Bloom's level 2: Understand), or you might promise them that they will be able to write a basic game-playing program (Bloom's level 3: Apply). In a class discussing a famous paper, you might promise that they will better understand what makes a paper great (Bloom's level 5: Evaluate).

For more on delivering an empowerment promise, see page 143.

See *How to Deliver a Lecture* (page 143) for examples of particular ways to deliver your promise.

Questions stimulate engagement

In many fields, instructors teach as Socrates did: read and then come to class to discuss what they have read. The instructor asks questions, and the students answer them.

When I teach such a class, I cover my copy of the reading assignment with highlighter, marginal notes, big question marks, and repeated explanation points. That markup provides the raw material for framing questions that address my empowerment promise.

In 1950, Alan Turing introduced what has come to be called the Turing test: an interrogator asks a computer and a person questions; each tries to answer as a person would; all interaction is via typed text; if an average interrogator has no better than a 70% chance of guessing correctly which responses are from the person after five minutes, then the computer can be said to be intelligent (Turing, 1950).

My copy of Turing's paper is full of markup, from which I extracted questions for a class.

- Do you think a machine that passes the Turing test necessarily sheds light on human intelligence?
- Is it always best to use all the arguments you can think of for or against a position?
- What do you think of the argument that computers can do only what they have been programmed to do?
- Why did Turing believe in extrasensory perception?

In a discussion-grounded class, everything centers on the questions and answers, but formulating good questions helps force engagement even in lectures. In *How to Deliver a Lecture* (page 143), you learn how to ask your questions in a manner that avoids perpetually averted eyes.

Powerful ideas expose the big picture

Seymour Papert, the inventor of the Logo programming language for children, made everyone around him smarter—from children to colleagues—by encouraging people to focus on the big picture and zero in on the powerful ideas. You can do the same for your students by highlighting how the material you teach generalizes to powerful ideas with wide applicability.

My way of highlighting is to put the powerful ideas up on a board before class begins, marked by big gold stars. When I talk about game-playing programs, two gold-star ideas emerge.

Gold star ideas.

The fail-fast principle dictates that programs should never explore moves that cannot possibly be best; an anytime algorithm is a program with the property that it provides an instant answer, but given more time, may produce a better answer.

Powerful ideas are what you need when you analyze, evaluate, and create. Thus, with a discussion of powerful ideas, you offer instruction at the three highest levels of Bloom's taxonomy.

For more on Bloom's taxonomy, see page 132.

Class size matters

What you do in a class depends on class size. If the student count is one to five, you can just converse; if five to 25, you can discuss assigned reading. Preparation time centers on reading the paper plus an hour or two thinking up questions to ask. If I have taught the class before, I read the paper again and then spend an hour on review and renewal.

If your class is too large for a discussion, or the subject does not lend itself to discussion, you are lecturing. If the student count is more than about 70, your lecture becomes theater and you are a performer. You are not just an instructor, you are a personality. Each student looks around, sees that there are many others, and expects you to have invested preparation time in proportion to class size.

Be ready for awkward moments

Someone socially immature may do something meant to taunt you. It may be a sexist or racist or xenophobic remark. It may be a project presentation that unexpectedly introduces an off-color theme. You need to know what to do in advance because there will be no time to think it through when the awful moment occurs. Here are some starting points:

- I'm sure you did not intend to be offensive, but you need to know that a lot of people, including me, find remarks like that to be extremely offensive.

- You must have known that I would find that remark to be offensive. I think you should reflect on what you have just done before you say something like that again.

- I take it that you intended that remark to be deliberately offensive because stupidity on that order is not in nature. [Adapted from Samuel Johnson's remark about Thomas Sheridan, also known as Sherry (Womersley, 2008)].

For more on walking out, see page 151.

In an extreme case, you can use the nuclear option. You can ask the offender to leave, and if the offender does not, then you can walk out.

Lecture preparation involves extra steps

All classes benefit from thought devoted to reflection on learning outcomes and on developing empowerment promises, questions, and powerful ideas. Preparation to lecture, especially to large audiences, requires more, often a lot more.

Allocate adequate preparation time

Each lecture I prepare from scratch takes me on average 20 hours to prepare. Colleagues report both more and less; somewhat more if the material is particularly difficult, somewhat less if they use notes or slides when they teach.

For more on a sample demonstration program, see page 145.

Then there is the matter of demonstrations. A demonstration can add a week because my demonstrations are programs that I generally write myself.

Occasionally, I exploit a shortcut. If I want to introduce new material, and a friend is an expert on the subject, I ask said friend in to do a lecture or two. I take notes furiously. Then, all I need to do is retell the story in my own voice, perhaps putting in a new promise at the beginning, adjusting the examples, clarifying the explanations, and adding a new way of concluding. This approach generally gets the average preparation time down to 10 hours.

I also may study someone's textbook or online course occasionally, and that too can cut down on preparation time, but not as much, and with some frustration, because those sources are not packaged to fill a 50-minute MIT time slot.

If I have done a lecture a few times before, then preparation is just a matter of review, renewal, and rehearsal.

Of course if you are at a place where you teach multiple subjects, you do not have 20 hours to prepare a lecture. You may get help from the publisher of the textbook. For subjects with large enrollments, publishers supply all kinds of outlines, notes, and slides. You should focus on removing some of the supplied slides, adding others, getting rid of the excess words, and deciding where you want to turn off the projector and work the boards.

For more on problems with publisher's slides, see page 148.

Select the examples

As you develop notes on what you want to talk about conceptually, you should look for examples to illustrate the concepts. I use some examples unaltered, I adapt others, and I work out still others myself.

Invariably, the examples involve drawings because we humans think with our eyes, not just with our mouths and ears. In a lecture on search programs, for example, I talk about finding a path from city S to city G.

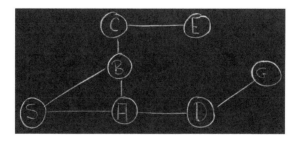

A simple search problem. A program is to find a path between the starting point, S, and the goal, G.

I point out that the example is so simple, I can readily sketch out all possible paths that contain no loops. Then, those paths serve as the foundation for discussing various search techniques, such as depth-first search and breadth-first search.

Depth-first search dives into the tree of paths, continuing until a dead end forces retreat to a place with an unexplored option. Breadth-first search plods along, layer by layer, looking for a complete path.

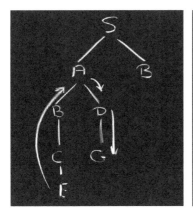 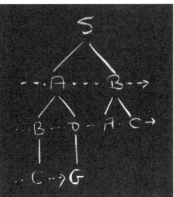

With those two searches described, the lecture continues to explain various kinds of search for the shortest path.

Work out the details

If your subject involves mathematics, you can sketch out any mathematics you want to discuss as you develop your examples. I always set up the mathematics with a drawing. Here is the drawing I use to show what can happen when a brute-force game-playing program looks at the moves available to a game player; then considers the moves that player's opponent can make; then considers the player's response to those opponent moves, and so on, down to a depth d.

A uniform game tree in which each game player has b moves available at each level for every situation at the previous level.

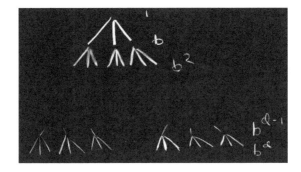

For each of the resulting b situations at level one, there are b possible responses, producing b^2 situations. Generalizing, at level d, there are b^d situations.

I point out that if b is 30 and each player makes 40 moves, both reasonable assumptions, then you cannot explore all the ways a chess game could develop.

Why? I work out the mathematics and show that even if all the atoms in the universe were fast computers, working together ever since the Big Bang, almost all of the ways a chess game could develop would remain unexplored!

Make an outline

Once you have decided on concepts, examples, and mathematics, if any, you are almost done. It is time to decide on order via an outline. I always use the broken-glass outline style.

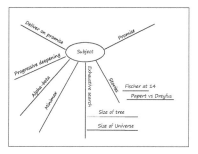

Initial outline for a lecture on games.

As preparation continues, I make adjustments and add details.

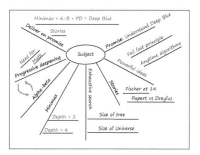

Final outline for a lecture on games, with expanded promise and delivery spokes, along with an added spoke for powerful ideas. Arrows indicate ordering swap.

Rehearse

In my Artificial Intelligence subject, I generally lecture to 350–400 students, which puts my classes well into the theater category. Just as I would not try to play Macbeth in *Macbeth* without rehearsal, I cannot imagine going into a big lecture hall without rehearsing.

First of five rehearsal boards for a lecture on game-playing programs. Note reference date on first board above an outline showing where the class lies in the subject and the structure of the current class.

My great good luck is that my lectures are at 10:00 am and my building, the Stata Center, has huge blackboards in community space. For my final rehearsal session, I get to those boards by 7:00 am, long before most of my students wake up.

I do not work in real time. Some material I go over quickly, faster than real time. Other material I stare at for many minutes, talking to myself, working out exactly what I want to say, often putting in a clarification I had never thought of before. If mathematics is involved or if the example is complex, I write it down, erase it, and do it again, just to be sure it is firmly in mind.

I also plan out where colored chalk can add clarity to the drawings. I think about how to arrange the drawings when I work with blackboards that slide up and down.

The net result is that I have the content memorized without particular effort. I do not mean word-for-word of course, but I do mean I can do the lecture without referring to notes. I have rehearsal-board pictures with me, of course, as a safety net, but I have not used them in years.

When I finish rehearsing, I photograph the boards for future reference; then, when I prepare for a lecture I have done before, I look over the pictures of the previous year's rehearsal boards and write what I see, usually with improvements, on the current year's rehearsal boards.

There is a daycare center in the Stata Center, the place where I practice, so little kids pass by, often offering various insights.

On some days, I can use all the help I can get.

What you need to know

When you prepare to instruct, you should develop a ritual that suits your style. You should include the following steps:

- Decide what you want your students to learn. Use Bloom's taxonomy or one of your own devising.
- Develop an empowerment promise and engagement-stimulating questions.
- Identify powerful ideas, so you teach more than skills.
- Ensure that your approach works with your class size.
- Be ready to handle sexist, racist, or xenophobic situations.
- Learn the material, with special attention to concepts, examples, and in science and engineering, the mathematics.
- Devise or select examples and work out the details.
- Prepare a broken-glass outline to help you organize your material.
- Rehearse, just as you would if you were acting in a play.

Where you can learn more

Karen Kelsky, in *The Professor Is In: The Essential Guide to Turning Your Ph.D. into a Job* (2015), explains how to succeed in academia and asks whether you want to do what you need to do.

*It usually takes me more than three weeks
to prepare a good impromptu speech.*

Commonly attributed to Samuel Clemens, also known
as Mark Twain; American writer and humorist

15 How to Deliver a Lecture

In this chapter, you learn to start a lecture with an empowerment promise. You also learn the merits of chalk on a board relative to slides on a screen and why you should ban mobile phones and laptops. Finally, you learn to stop by delivering on your promise.

Live lectures remain popular

Recorded lectures have obvious advantages. They need not fit into a standard time slot. Students can speed them up. Students can listen again to parts they did not fully understand. Students can spend time in flipped classrooms.

For more on flipped classrooms, see page 131.

Because many of my lectures are online, I wonder why students come to look at photons bouncing off of me. Some tell me they watch the online video and then come to class anyway.

Perhaps it is a social phenomenon. Perhaps there is something mysteriously special about watching a live performance, much like the mysteriously special enjoyment you have when you go to a play or concert.

Start with your empowerment promise

Everyone who comes to your lecture wants to know if listening to you talk will be worthwhile. Accordingly, you need to convince everyone that they are better off spending an hour with you than reading their email, texting their friends, or surfing the web. That is, you need to promise everyone in your audience some kind of empowerment.

Empowerment comes in many forms. Students will feel empowered if they can work the problems or do well on the examinations. Academics will feel empowered if they see a problem in a new light. Voters, if they like what they hear. Investors, if they learn about new ways to make money. And everyone will feel empowered if something is learned that will be a good topic for dinner conversation.

You need to deliver your empowerment promise right away, certainly within the first five minutes.

Promise via an outline

To deliver an empowerment promise in a lecture, you can write on your blackboard an outline of what you plan to do. That has the desirable feature that it tells your audience that you are about to start as well as serving as a vehicle for delivering on your promise. The emergence of the outline says it is time to terminate conversations, stop texting, and quit reading email.

Here is the outline I put up for the first lecture in my Artificial Intelligence subject.

A sample lecture outline. The outline includes a promise that each student will understand what Artificial Intelligence is about by the end of the lecture.

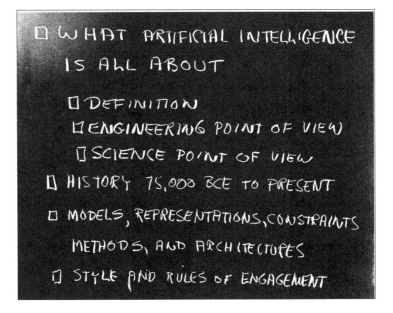

Promise via a system demonstration

To express an empowerment promise, you can demonstrate a system that will be understood. One of my lectures in my Artificial Intelligence subject is about how to search for a path from one place to another. I point out that search is everywhere; you need search not only to drive from one city to another, but also to solve problems, to allocate resources, and to deal with stories.

I explain that finding a way to color a map of the United States, without assigning the same color to states with a common border, illustrates the key ideas. Then, within the first few minutes, I demonstrate a search program that finds a way to color all the states with just red, green, yellow, and blue.

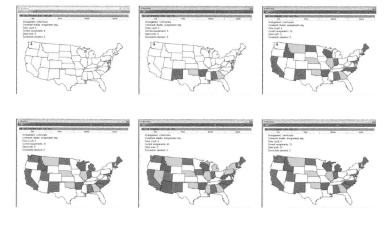

A simple search program in action. Texas causes trouble, as it is colored last, and no colors are left.

Video available via QR code:

I note that no one will want to wait for the program to finish, because the search for colors is awkwardly arranged, and it will take greatly in excess of 1,000 years for the simple program to finish.

But, I say, by the end of the hour, you will know how to write a program that does the work in a few seconds. If you have any interest at all in Artificial Intelligence, that is empowering.

Use boards to teach

When students offer teaching feedback at MIT, they often say "More chalk, fewer slides."

When you use a blackboard or whiteboard, the material flows out at about the speed at which the audience can absorb it. Students not only see it, they also have time to think about it. There is, as the electrical engineers say, a good impedance match.

Speed may not be the only answer to why boards are better. Another answer may involve *mirror neurons*—those neurons in our heads that are active both when we do something and when we watch someone else do that same thing.

The purpose of mirror neurons remains a controversial mystery, but it seems clear that watching someone write differs from seeing the same words in type on a slide. At some level, we feel ourselves empathetically writing when we see someone write; we do not when we see something already written.

Which are better, blackboards or whiteboards? I prefer blackboards. I like the substantial feel of one-inch railroad chalk in my hand and I like how it feels to write with it. I do not like whiteboard markers; they feel flimsy, produce anemic lines, smell bad, and always seem to run out of ink at inopportune moments.

Old-fashioned, one-inch diameter, railroad chalk remains a terrific teaching tool.

I also prefer boards to electronic projection from a tablet. It may be because working on a tablet in a large room gives little stimulation to the listener's motor neurons.

When I ask colleagues who lecture exclusively with slides why they do it, they say it is because they can cover more material.

They confuse covering more material with teaching more material.

Cannot get enough on a slide? Use a smaller font. Cannot get enough on 25 slides? Press the remote-control's advance key faster.

For more on reading slides, see page 86.

Giving a lecture with slides makes it easy to lecture, especially if all you do is go to class and read what is on a screen out loud. Then, you put all those slides on the web and wonder why students stop showing up. It is because students can read and do not need you to read to them.

The context for my philippic against slides is university-level teaching. Most corporate training aims more to expose ideas than to teach listeners learning at an examination-taking level. Slides are the right vehicle for exposing ideas.

Use block capitals; eschew cursive writing

I went to a lot of trouble practicing cursive writing in elementary school. Too bad; I never became good at it. My block capital writing is much easier to read. Probably yours is, too.

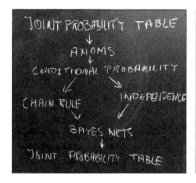

Block capital writing is easier to read than cursive.

Use slides as condiments

Although I mostly write on a blackboard, I often use slides as condiments, especially in the beginning of a lecture in connection with the empowerment promise, and at the end, when I deliver on the promise.

When I start a lecture on IBM's Deep Blue chess-playing program, the first to beat a human champion, I talk about the famous debate, in the late 1960s, between Hubert Dreyfus (against) and Seymour Papert (for) about whether computers can be made to play chess at a championship level.

Then, at the end of the lecture, having pointed out that listeners now understand the fundamentals of how Deep Blue played chess, I talk about the famous match in 1963 between Bobby Fischer, age 14, and grand master Robert Byrne, which Fischer wins by a queen sacrifice.

Deep Blue could have seen value in that queen sacrifice only if it could look ahead 21 levels, which would have taken Deep Blue about 50 years.

Beware of slides supplied by textbook publishers

For more on
publisher's lecture
slides, see page 137.

Many publishers of high-volume textbooks offer resources to busy instructors. Typically, the publishers offer examinations, workbooks, and lecture slides.

For more on bullet
lists, see page 91.

That offer of slide sets sounds great until you look at the slides. I once opened a sample slide set that covered the material in one chapter of a widely used computer-science textbook. I found 78 slides. Four slides included not-very-good illustrations copied from figures in the textbook. The rest were tiresome bullet lists.

If you are so busy you must use such slides, try to find time to reduce the word count.

Fictitious resource
slide and a quick
revision to get rid of
excess words. The
revised slide could be
revealed, one line at a
time, enabling you to
focus on each line as
it is revealed.

Definition of Artificial Intelligence	WHAT AI IS ALL ABOUT
• First and foremost, Artificial intelligence is about perception, thinking, and action. • The key idea is to make models, so that we can understand how things work computationally. • To make a good model, you need a good representation. • The essence of a good representation is that a good representation exposes constraint. • Once you have constraints in hand, you can devise algorithms that exploit the constraints. • Finally, you can package up all your algorithms using one of the standard architectures.	Models of perception, thinking, and action supported by representations that expose constraints that enable algorithms deployed by architectures
LOTS OF WORDS PUBLISHING **POWERED LEARNING**	

For more on reading
slides, see page 86.

In the form as given by the fictitious publisher, Lots of Words Publishing, the slide invites reading, but reading slides as you instruct invites sleep and absenteeism. And because no one can listen to you and read densely worded slides at the same time, you might as well not be there. Just have a teaching assistant silently advance through the slides fast enough to get through all of them in the allocated time.

For more on review
copies, see page 88.

If you plan to provide slides to students for study after you instruct, you might think that your slides need more words, not fewer. You can escape from both Scylla and Charybdis by posting the slides you take from the original wordy set and instructing with your revised, more telegraphic adaptations.

Force engagement by asking questions

For more on
preparation, see
page 135.

Your preparation should include developing a set of interesting questions designed to engage the students.

Use the Rumpelstiltskin maneuver

If you ask, "How much is 2 + 2?" you will see nothing but blank stares and averted eyes. Students feel foolish answering questions that are too simple. On the other end, if you ask a too-hard question, you will also see nothing but blank stares and averted eyes.

If you ask a question that is not too easy and not too hard, you are still likely to see nothing but averted eyes and blank stares, some from students who fear ridicule if their answer is wrong, some from students who do not want to seem to be seeking favor, some from students who are simply shy.

There are, however, easy ways to ensure response. One is to remember your students' names; then you can ask, "Well, x, what do you think?"

I call it the Rumpelstiltskin maneuver, recalling the fairy tale about a miller's daughter who gained power over an imp by learning his name. You will get power over your students if you know their names. There will be no averted eyes because they soon learn that averted eyes make them attractive targets for the question just asked.

I memorize my students' names with picture-and-name flash cards, which enable me to learn the names of 50 students without much trouble. In a large class, with several hundred students, I generally manage to memorize the names of about 80% of the students. When I greet one of those students by name somewhere on campus, the student is amazed and more likely to be engaged in class.

An alternative to memorizing names, much practiced in business schools, requires students to bring nameplates to class.

Use the puzzle-and-poll maneuver

Another way to promote engagement is to present an interesting puzzle and do a poll. My colleague Andrew Lo, a brilliant financial economist and fantastic instructor, likes to present the following puzzle, a chart showing return on a dollar invested in each of four assets over an 18-year period.

Past asset performance. Of A, B, C, and D, which would you choose now, based on past performance? Image courtesy of Andrew Lo.

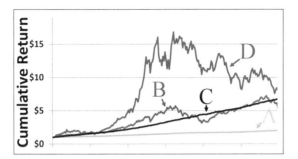

"Who would invest in asset A?" he asks, then proceeding to ask who would invest in asset B, C, or D. Almost all in the audience become engaged; almost all choose asset C on the ground that it returns about 10% annually with little worrisome volatility.

Asset A is US Treasury Bills; asset B is the US stock market; asset D is Pfizer, a pharmaceutical company. Alas, asset C, the one most people choose, was one of the funds involved in the Bernie Madoff Ponzi scheme, which ended up cheating thousands of investors out of billions of dollars. In his seminal book, *Adaptive Markets: Financial Evolution at the Speed of Thought* (2017), Lo describes how it all happened, noting that what seemed too good to be true was in fact too good to be true. A dollar invested in asset C in 1990 became more than six dollars by October 2008; a month later Madoff was arrested and the investments still in his funds became worthless.

The time axis on the chart is unlabeled; guessers are more likely to pick C when they do not know that the time period ends during the global financial crisis of 2008.

Be inclusive

Remind yourself to engage broadly. Otherwise, a class of 25 can turn into a discussion among three or four.

Invite argument

You can execute, especially in a small class, a variant on the puzzle-and-poll maneuver in which you ask people to solve puzzles working together. As soon as released to work together, a class animates itself. Many students start gesturing, some draw diagrams, often arguments erupt.

Consider technology-enabled polling

Some instructors like to outfit students with clickers so that students can respond to questions electronically. Instructors then view poll results instantly and perhaps display the results on a screen. If there are many wrong answers, instructors respond with more explanation or by asking students with the right answer to convince the others.

One obvious advantage is that clicker polling does not embarrass shy students fearful of ridicule if they choose the wrong answer. One not-so-obvious advantage is that instructors who choose to have clickers feel obligated to use them, and so must conceive interesting and informing polling questions.

Encourage engagement via note-taking

Sitting passively, listening to a rapidly moving lecture, encourages both sleep and wandering thoughts. I tell my students to combat those natural tendencies by taking notes. They need not look at their notes afterward; they write down key ideas and draw diagrams so as to force concentration. You cannot take notes without engaging your symbolic and perceptual faculties.

Ban mobile phones, open laptops, and other distracting devices

When I learned about circuit theory as an MIT undergraduate, Professor Amar Bose, who later founded Bose Corporation, lectured. Electrical engineering sophomores sat at two-person tables, equipped with—hard to believe today—colorful stamped-aluminum ash trays.

In those days, students often made a hissing noise, like a snake, whenever an instructor announced a quiz or told a particularly corny joke. Bose didn't like it; he considered it insulting. On the first day of class, he announced there would be no hissing.

A few weeks later, somebody hissed. Bose said that whoever hissed would have to leave, and the student left. Then, a lecture or two later, early in the lecture, someone hissed again. But this time the culprit refused to identify himself. So Bose left, and that lecture was gone forever. Those who knew the hisser or sat close to him gave him a pretty hard time. Nobody hissed in Bose's class again.

We all knew Bose respected us because he put so much effort into teaching. We respected him because he did not put up with what he considered insults. Mutual respect is the stuff from which great education emerges.

Inspired by Bose, I do not allow students in my lectures to use mobile phones or laptops while I lecture. It distracts them and studies have shown it distracts those around them (Sana et al., 2013). It also would distract me, lowering the quality of my lecture, affecting everyone.

Deliver on your promise

You want everyone to think that listening to you is worthwhile, so it is important to deliver on your initial promise.

Demonstrate success

You can do a demonstration. For example, the fast program assigns one of four colors to all the states, without assigning bordering states the same color, in just a few seconds.

A sophisticated search program at work.

Video available via QR code:

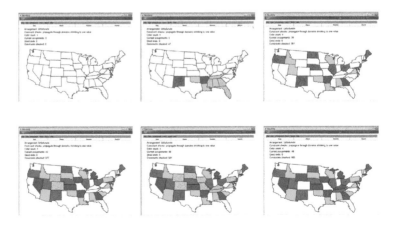

With such a demonstration, you show that you have delivered: "So, there you have it; now you know how to write an efficient search program that takes just seconds to do what would otherwise take millennia."

Tell a story

Donald Sadoway taught 3.091, Solid State Chemistry, in the same lecture hall where I teach my Artificial Intelligence subject. He had the lecture hall for the hour before me, so I had the opportunity to see the final five minutes or so of all his lectures.

Sadoway always ends his lectures with a story. His lecture on the structure of DNA, for example, concludes with the story of how Rosalind Franklin was denied, by sexism and death, a much-deserved part of the Nobel prize awarded for determining the structure of DNA, one of the great scientific achievements of the 20th century.

Sadoway explains how Rosalind Franklin was denied proper recognition for her work on the structure of DNA. Video courtesy of Donald Sadoway.

Video available via QR code:

Show commitment

For many years, Walter Lewin taught 8.01, Classical Mechanics. Much admired for his teaching at MIT, he often ended his lectures with demonstrations.

Lewin testifies to his belief in the conservation of energy. Video courtesy of Walter Lewin.

Video available via QR code:

In a lecture recorded in 1999, Lewin took his life into his own hands, trusting in the conservation of energy, confident that a large steel ball, swinging on a wire attached to the ceiling, would not crush his head.

When I took 8.01, much earlier, Alan Lazarus performed the same demonstration. I still remember it. You cannot help but think, "Well, he really, really believes in this stuff."

Warning! Do not try this at home. Even physics lecturers sometimes fail to suppress the instinct to push, thereby putting enough extra energy into the ball that it causes serious damage on return.

Embellish with a joke

After you have delivered on your empowerment promise, you can embellish your lecture with something light, which is an especially good idea if the material is difficult.

Once, I was having a glass of wine with my friend Douglas Lenat, founder of Cycorp, who is a fantastic speaker. I asked, "What makes you so admired as a speaker?"

"Oh," he replied, "I always finish with a joke. That way everyone in the audience thinks they have had fun the whole time."

What you need to know

To lecture successfully, you must adhere to a few imperatives:

- Start with an empowerment promise, expressed perhaps via an outline or a demonstration.
- Recognize that boards are for teaching ideas; slides are for exposing ideas.
- Write with block capitals to maximize legibility.
- Maintain respect: ban mobile phones and laptops.
- Be inclusive.
- Encourage engagement by recommending note-taking.
- Ask questions and force engagement by calling on specific students, by running a poll, by demanding that people work together, and by encouraging argument.
- When you stop, note that you have delivered on your promise.
- Embellish with a concluding demonstration, joke, or story.

Where you can learn more

Noted educator James M. Lang, in *Small Teaching: Everyday Lessons from the Science of Learning* (2016), explains how you can get big learning improvements through small changes. He argues convincingly, and backed by a great deal of research, for various ways of encouraging engagement. He recommends, for example, posing provocative questions, asking for predictions about a problem to be studied, and telling stories.

...Give me that man
That is not passion's slave, and I will wear him
In my heart's core, ay, in my heart of heart.

William Shakespeare; English poet, playwright, and actor

From *Hamlet*, Act III, Scene 2, Lines 1950–1952
Open Source Shakespeare (Shakespeare, 1600)

16 How to Inspire

In this chapter, you learn what various people consider to be inspiring. In particular, you learn that expressed passion is a key ingredient of inspiring instruction.

There are many kinds of inspiration

A few years ago, Anantha Chandrakasan, then my department's head, asked me to talk with incoming faculty in MIT's School of Engineering about lecturing. "Sure," I said, and then he said, "Be sure to tell them how to be inspiring."

I have studied lecturing for a long time, and I had ideas about how to start, how to stop, and everything in between, but somehow I had never thought specifically about how to be inspiring.

I decided to ask around, talking about inspiration with incoming freshmen, undergraduates, graduate students, junior faculty, and senior faculty. "Who has inspired you and how?" I asked.

I soon learned there were several kinds of responses. The incoming freshmen talked about high-school teachers who gave them confidence by telling them they could do what they never dreamed that they could do. Senior faculty talked about people who had shown them a new way of looking at a problem. Some talked about their admiration for people who have shown unstoppable optimism in the face of almost certain disaster.

I learned that *inspiration* is one of those words Marvin Minsky called *suitcase words* (Minsky, 2006). Each suitcase word is a label for so many ideas that it is like a suitcase so big you can stuff almost anything into it. *Inspiration, intelligence, creativity,* and *emotion* are such many-meaning words.

So, when you talk to people about inspiration, there will be diversity, but nevertheless, most people agree on one characteristic: people inspire when they exhibit passion for what they do.

Inspiration flows from observed passion

When I graduated from MIT with an SB in Electrical Engineering, I really had no idea what I wanted to do. I found myself the following year in graduate school, but did not know why. My father muttered, darkly, about law school.

Then, a friend dragged me to one of Marvin Minsky's lectures. The lecture described a program, written by James R. Slagle, that solved calculus problems in a manner much like an MIT freshman would solve such problems.

Minsky's lectures inspired me to develop a computational account of human intelligence. Image of Minsky speaking at the General Motors Research Laboratory in 1968 courtesy of Gerald Jay Sussman.

The lecture was not particularly clear or organized, and it certainly was not practiced, but clearly Minsky was passionate about the idea that a computer could do advanced mathematical manipulation. As I walked out, I said to my friend, "I want to do what he does." I was inspired.

Exhibit your passion explicitly

How do you let your students know you are passionate about what you are teaching? One way is to just tell them:

> There you have it, a program that tells us *Macbeth* is about *revenge* and *Pyrrhic victory*. What could be cooler than that!

> So there it is, a program that can be said, in a suitcase word way, to be self-aware. I think that is interesting beyond description!

> No doubt about it, 99% of your DNA is the same as that of a chimpanzee. I can tell you without a doubt that I think that 1% must be pretty important!

> Picasso painted *Guernica* in response to the 1937 destruction of a Basque village in northern Spain by Nazi German and Fascist Italian bombers. I cannot think how anyone could look at the painting without feeling its incredible anti-war message!

> Words matter, and Kennedy's words mattered a lot. In 1962, he said we would go to the moon in that decade, and we did. It was a masterpiece! It inspired the nation! It inspired me!

But what if you are not passionate about what you are teaching. Maybe it is boring stuff everyone has to know, but it is not intrinsically interesting. If so, you better not tell anyone. Telling students something is not interesting is fatal.

One highly respected, highly effective colleague said to me, "You know, there is some stuff I have to teach that really is boring. Before I teach it, I have to psych up for an hour, telling myself it is interesting, so I can at least go to class and pretend it is interesting."

Another colleague, also highly respected and highly effective, told me that she spends a lot of time working up interesting metaphors on the ground that interesting metaphors can make uninteresting material become interesting.

What you need to know

Inspiration is different from teaching, and perhaps more important. To be inspiring, you can:

- Assure young people they can do what they did not know they could do.
- Tell not-so-young people how to look at a problem in a new way.
- Show passion for what you are talking about. Say that it excites you and keeps you awake at night.

Where you can learn more

Ken Bain, in *What the Best College Teachers Do*, argues that the best teachers focus on learning objectives and conspicuously display passion for the material they teach and trust in the students who are to learn it (Bain, 2004).

Part IV
Writing

The gods help them that help themselves.

Ancient Greek proverb

17 How to Write to Be Understood

In this chapter, you learn about key elements that draw seasoned readers into reading what you write and that help all readers to understand what you are trying to say. You also learn that when you write, you should supply those key elements.

Good readers deploy reading heuristics

Some people seem to read everything. Thomas Knight, one of the founders of synthetic biology, is one of them, and in biology, even in narrow subfields, the literature is vast.

"Tom," I said, "You seem to read everything. How do you find the time?"

"Oh," he said, "I just look at the illustrations and read the captions."

He explained that if a paper contains an important idea, the author would be sure to provide an illustration that exposes it, not necessarily consciously, but almost certainly. Then, if the exposed idea seems important, Tom examines the paper more carefully.

Everyone has to develop ways to get the sense of what a paper contributes, if anything, from clues that lie on the surface. You have no time to read a paper unless it seems to contribute something you think is important.

Authors hallucinate that their writing is clear

Authors understand what they are writing about, so it never occurs to them that much is left out, much is unclear, and much motivation is missing. They have their papers read by colleagues and students who also understand the subject matter well, so they, too, hallucinate that the writing is complete, clear, and motivated.

Reading such a paper frustrates. You have to piece together what the Contributions are, but the Contributions, if any, are implicit.

Seasoned readers extract
the essence from surface clues

Because there is too much to read, and most of it is poorly written, you have to develop tools for rapid decryption.

Read the abstract

Well-written abstracts tell you what you will learn from the paper. Unfortunately, many abstracts come up short of well written.

Read the introduction

In many papers, the introduction repeats the abstract verbatim. In better papers, the introduction expands on what you find in the abstract, and the additional detail helps you to decide whether to go further.

Examine the conclusion

For more on Conclude with Contributions, see page 11.

Many authors conclude with a conclusion section. If so, with luck, you may learn what a paper is about and what it contributes. If an author sensibly concludes with a section titled *Contributions*, that author probably read the section of this book titled *Conclude with Contributions*.

Note the section titles

Some authors deploy instructive, full-sentence section titles. I used the following examples in a paper that describes how a program that treats a story as a connected sequence of event descriptions can make a better summary than a program that treats a story as a bag of words (Winston, 2015).

Vision: Good story summary requires story understanding

The Genesis system models human story-understanding

The Genesis system enables high-quality story summary

Other authors use vacuous titles that serve only as separators:

Introduction

Conclusions

Such section titles squander a decryption opportunity.

Note, however, that some fields have evolved standardized section titles, such as *Methods*, *Results*, and *Discussion*.

For more on standardized section titles, see page 171.

Look at the illustrations and read the captions

Knight is right. The illustrations and captions reveal essential content. The following example is from *Amorphous Computing*, a paper that Knight co-authored (Abelson et al., May 2000).

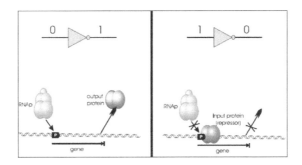

The two idealized cases for a biological inverter. If the input repressor is absent, RNAP (RNA polymerase) transcribes the gene for the output protein and enables its synthesis. If the input repressor is present, no output protein is synthesized. Image courtesy of Thomas Knight.

Look at the lists

Lists draw readers' eyes. Lists have value because they help readers find essential elements such as these:

- An identification of alternatives, as in this list itself.
- An articulation of Steps, as in what the writer has done.
- An articulation of Steps, as in what the writer wants the reader to do.
- A recital of commitments, as in what a proposer promises to do.
- A summary, as in identification of what the reader needs to know or do.
- A summary, as in identification of Contributions.

If you use lists with bullets, you should use them sparingly so that they retain their eye-drawing force. Using too many bullet lists has a mind-numbing effect.

Some authors do not like bullet lists and never use them at all in their written work, preferring to write out lists with *First, ..., Second, ..., Third, ...,* markers. Such authors note that bullet lists have at least two problems: first, bullet lists look ugly and jarring to some readers; second, bullet lists look especially ugly and jarring whenever the items are longer than a one-line phrase or sentence.

Check the citations

You develop a sense of who is in the author's research community by whom the author cites. That is why I despise citation by number [88].[1] To figure out who is cited, you have to look at the bibliography, which takes time and distracts.[2]

You should cite by name, so the reader knows whom you reference, and by year, so the reader knows when the referenced work was published, as in (Einstein, 1905).

Edward R. Tufte, *The Visual Display of Quantitative Information*, Graphics Press, 2001.

Tufte (2001), idiosyncratically, puts each citation, fully, in the margins of his books. Tufte's practice has much to recommend it, as it tells you right away the title as well as the author and year.

Read summary paragraphs and skim the topic sentences

Some authors know their material is difficult and show they care by including short summaries at the end of every section. Shimon Ullman's book, *High Level Vision* (1996), is full of helpful summaries such as this (page 293):

> In summary, one way of shifting the processing focus around in the course of applying visual routines is by first extracting a set of distinguished locations in the scene,

---

[1] 88 is an example; 88 identifies nothing in the bibliography.

[2] In general, footnotes are overused. Avoid them because reading them requires the reader to make a judgment about whether they want to read about material not sufficiently important to merit inclusion in the main text. Many, perhaps most of them, are included at the last moment to address comments by reviewers.

and then shifting the processing focus towards one of these locations....

On another level, you should remember what you were no doubt told in high school: start most paragraphs with a topic sentence that tells you what the paragraph is about. Such authors are much to be honored because they enable skimming.

Provide the surface clues readers need

Once you know how seasoned readers will read what you write, it follows that you should be sure to provide what they look for, such as good illustrations and captions, instructive section titles, meaningful citations, thoughtful lists, and summary paragraphs.

You should be sure to summarize what you have done in your abstract and introduction, paying particular attention to the *Vision*, *Steps*, *News*, and *Contributions* elements discussed in *Essentials of Persuasion* (page 7). To take clarity to an even higher level, you should replace your introduction section with three sections titled *Vision*, *Steps*, and *News*, and you should replace your Conclusion section with a section titled *Contributions*.

Then, when you think you are done, have your paper read by a friend. Choose a friend who is not so close to what you do that the friend, like you, will hallucinate that your work is complete, clear, and well motivated.

What you need to know

When you write, you should exploit what you know about how seasoned readers read what you have written. In particular, you should:

- Write an abstract that helps readers decide if they want more. Include, in summary form, your Vision, Steps, News, and Contributions.

- Start with introductory sections detailing your Vision and Steps and citing some News, thus adding detail to what you say in the abstract.

- Write a conclusion describing your contributions; title it *Contributions*.
- Capture the key ideas in illustrations with self-explanatory captions.
- Use full sentence, self-summarizing section titles.
- Include author names and publication dates in citations.
- Use lists to call attention to alternatives, steps, and summary points.
- Include summaries at the end of each section.
- Use topic sentences liberally.
- Have your papers read for clarity by someone not already familiar with what you do.

See *Essentials of Persuasion* (page 7) for more discussion on Vision, Steps, News, and Contributions, all of which should be prominent in what you write.

Writing a book is not unlike building a house or planning a battle or painting a picture. The technique is different, the materials are different, but the principle is the same. The foundations have to be laid, the data assembled, and the premises must bear the weight of their conclusions. Ornaments or refinements may then be added.

Winston S. Churchill; British statesman, writer, and Prime Minister

From *A Roving Commission: My Early Life* (Churchill, 1930), page 212

18 How to Organize Your Writing

In this chapter, you learn an overall strategy for writing that helps you focus on your contributions. The chapter builds on the outlining idea in *Essentials of Outlining* (page 29) and the persuasion ideas in *Essentials of Persuasion* (page 7). Subsequent chapters go into more detail about how to compose each of several standard sections.

Write the *Contributions* section first

Your paper should end with a section titled *Contributions*. If you cannot think of any Contributions, you are not ready to write the paper.

Do not title the final section *Conclusions*. You want your reader to know you have made contributions, not just observations. The right label enforces discipline on you and helps your reader to see you have done something. See *What to Put at the End* (page 183) for details.

For more on contributions, see page 11.

Optionally, prepare the illustrations

Some authors prepare their illustrations before they write. That way, much of the writing merely explains what is in the illustrations.

Add sections expected by your community

Many fields have community standards with respect to what is expected.

In a research paper, for example, you are expected to discuss related work, so you should include a section with the following title to make plain to your readers that you have done your duty:

- *Related work:* You explain the work of others, especially those whose work you extend and those whose work has inspired you. Highlight the novel characteristics of your own work, especially compared to other work that might seem superficially similar.

Similarly, many fields have expectations best met by including sections with titles such as these:

- *Goal:* You pose a goal, note why it is important, and explain how you will test whether you have succeeded in reaching it.
- *When and why:* You describe when your method works and why. You also describe when it does not work and why so as to inform future researchers.
- *Hypothesis:* You offer a hypothesis, note why it is interesting, and explain how you will test your hypothesis.

In the experimental sciences, community standards generally include:

- *Methods:* You supply a detailed description of how experiments were done so that others can reproduce the experiment and check the results. Many readers will skim or skip this section.
- *Results:* You describe what happened, often in the form of tables and graphs, without comment. Readers can draw their own conclusions.
- *Discussion:* You express your opinion about implications of your work, tie what you did to a larger picture, and, perhaps, suggest what to do next.

If you are writing a business plan for venture capitalists, then you are likely to want sections with titles such as these:

- *The opportunity:* You explain the problem you are solving, why customers will value your solution, how many customers will pay for it, and what they will pay.
- *Why now:* You explain, perhaps, that a window of opportunity has emerged because new technology has become available but large corporations, with much inertia, have not had time to seize the opportunity.

- *Why us:* You explain what makes you special, which may be that you have personally done research on how new technology solves a problem that people are willing to pay to have solved.

- *Competition barriers:* You describe your patents, trade secrets, prototypes, or other characteristics that make it hard for someone else to compete with you.

- *Key personnel:* You describe your experience and that of your team, with emphasis on past successes doing what you are proposing to do.

If you are writing a report on the work of a study group, formed to advise a sponsor, you likely will have these sections:

- *Executive summary:* You write one or two pages to be read by executives who are too busy to read your whole report.

- *Instructions from sponsor:* You include your sponsor's instructions, sometimes called *Terms of reference*, which generally includes a list of questions.

- *Members:* You identify who participated in your study.

- Sections mirroring each of the questions given in your instructions. Each includes findings.

- *Recommendations:* The actions you think your sponsor should take.

Write the *Vision, Steps,* and *News* sections next

See *What to Put at the Beginning* (page 177) for details.

Finally, write an abstract

See *How to Write an Abstract* (page 187) for details.

Optionally, write about the past

Many readers want to know what you have accomplished before wading through a detailed history of the problem, but some readers expect you to discuss prior work right away so that they can be sure you know your field and that you are, in fact, extending that which has come before.

One good compromise between early and late discussion of prior work is to include in your Vision section a paragraph that starts like this: "During the past n years, there has been much related work. In particular, the work reported here was inspired by and builds on the work of x, y, and z by showing that a, b, and c. In the penultimate section, the one labeled *Prior work*, I review the work of x, y, and z in detail along with other relevant literature."

Optionally, write about the future

Future work belongs to the future, but it is a bad idea to write about it at the end of your paper. That is where Contributions belong, because many readers decide whether to read a paper by reading the abstract and whatever is at the end. So put a section titled *Future work* just before the section titled *Contributions*.

If you have both a prior-work section and a future-work section, put prior work before future work.

Future-work sections, incidentally, are often the weakest part of a paper. Striking the future-work section would improve many papers because future-work sections tend to be filled with chores of little consequence that the authors had not yet done when they ran out of time.

Include acknowledgments according to convention

For more on saluting collaborators, see page 45.

Some journals want you to add acknowledgments as a kind of postscript at the end. Others have a footnote convention. Do what they want you to do, but be sure you have acknowledgments somewhere.

What you need to know

You will find writing easier if you have a strategy aimed at ensuring all important elements are included.

- Write the *Contributions* section first.
- Consider preparing your illustrations next.
- Add sections that fulfill community expectations.
- Add *Vision*, *Steps*, and *News* elements.
- Write an abstract.
- Include sections on prior work, future work, and acknowledgments, as needed.

Show your hand immediately!

Marvin Minsky; American scientist, professor, and pioneer in Artificial Intelligence

Frequent advice to students on presentation and writing

19 What to Put at the Beginning

In this chapter, you learn what you should write about in the beginning of your written work, so as to promote excitement and to convince readers that you know what you are doing. In particular, you learn about a set of standard openings that serve the purpose of getting you started, much like the standard openings chess masters use to get a game underway.

Start with your *Vision*

In *Essentials of Persuasion* (page 7), you learned that you should start a technical presentation, spoken or written, with your Vision.

You also learned that your Vision has two parts: a problem someone cares about and your approach to solving that problem.

You can express your Vision in a variety of ways, just as you can choose from many opening moves when playing chess. Various alternatives find their way into research papers, proposals, and business plans.

Identify your *Vision* with a community-specific heading

Because each community has community expectations, you should deploy a Vision heading that is community specific. It could be, for example, *Threat*, or *Opportunity*, or *Goal*, or *Hypothesis*.

For more on communities, see page 9.

For more on community expectations, see page 171.

Express your *Vision* with an *if-then* opening

The first opening to try, and the safety net if all else fails, is the *if-then* opening. The *if* part identifies the problem you are solving; the *then* part previews your approach:

> If we are to have a computational theory of human intelligence, then we should focus on what makes us different from other primates, living and extinct.

So, the problem is that we do not have a computational theory of human intelligence. The approach is to figure out what makes us different.

I use the *if-then* opening, but not always so conspicuously, because I tend to weave the *if* and the *then* into a story.

The problem is that we have no theory of human intelligence.

> Just about everyone agrees that much has been accomplished since Alan Turing published his seminal paper, *Computer Machinery and Intelligence.* (Turing, 1950) On the other hand, most would also agree that less has been accomplished than expected. Although applications of Artificial Intelligence are everywhere, we still do not have a computational theory of human intelligence. A team of dedicated first-class engineers can build systems that defeat skilled adults at chess and Jeopardy, but no one can build a system that exhibits the common sense of a child.
>
> ....
>
> What is missing, I think, is an approach centered on asking what exactly makes humans different from other primates and from early versions of ourselves. (Winston, 2011)

My approach is to ask what makes us different.

Express your *Vision* with an *interesting-story* opening

Your higher purpose may be to explain that which otherwise might be baffling, so your *Vision* section may tell a story about someone being baffled.

That was Marvin Minsky's purpose when he wrote his seminal paper, *Steps toward Artificial Intelligence.* He elected to start with an interesting story:

> A visitor to our planet might be puzzled about the role of computers in our technology. On the one hand, he would read and hear all about wonderful "mechanical brains" baffling their creators with prodigious intellectual performance. And he (or it) would be warned that these machines must be restrained, lest they overwhelm us by might, persuasion, or even by the revelation of truths too terrible to be borne. On the other hand, our

visitor would find the machines being denounced, on all sides, for their slavish obedience, unimaginative literal interpretations, and incapacity for innovation or initiative; in short, for their inhuman dullness.

....

Is this enough to justify so much interest, let alone deep concern? I believe that it is; that we are on the threshold of an era that will be strongly influenced, and quite possibly dominated, by intelligent problem-solving machines. But our purpose is not to guess about what the future may bring; it is only to try to describe and explain what seem now to be our first steps toward the construction of "artificial intelligence."

....

The literature does not include any general discussion of the outstanding problems of this field. In this article, an attempt will be made to separate out, analyze, and find the relations between some of these problems. (Minsky, 1961)

So, sorting out what Artificial Intelligence is all about is the problem someone cares about and the idea is to explain the structure of the new field.

Express your *Vision* with a *big-questions* opening

Your higher purpose may be to answer an important question, so your *Vision* section may articulate the question and what you propose to do about it.

Minsky opened his famous K-lines paper on the purpose of memory with a *big-questions* opening:

Most theories of memory suggest that when you learn or memorize something, a representation of that something is constructed, stored and later retrieved. This leads to questions like:
How is the information represented?
How is it stored?
How is it retrieved?
How is it used?
New situations are never exactly the same as old, so if

an old memory is to be useful, it must somehow be generalized or abstracted. This leads us also to ask:

How are the abstractions made?

When—before or after storage?

How are they later instantiated?

We try to deal with all these at once, via the thesis that *the function of a memory is to recreate a state of mind.* (Minsky, 1980)

So, eight big questions constitute the problem someone cares about and the thesis, "the function of a memory is to recreate a state of mind," constitutes the idea.

Express your *Vision* with a *mission-blocker* opening

There is a mission—something like selling your product, saving the planet, or protecting the country—and something stands in the way of accomplishing the mission. What is needed is your idea about how to remove the mission-blocking obstacle. Here is an example:

> Recent developments in Artificial Intelligence invite worry about whether intelligent but out-of-control systems will do us harm. To mitigate such dangers, it is important that we develop systems with humanlike ability to introspect into their own behavior and explain how they reach conclusions. (Winston and Holmes, 2018)

Express your *Vision* with a *new opportunity* opening

There is a long-standing, mission-critical problem, with a new solution. Here is a fanciful example:

> No one has time to look for a suitable spouse, and all the dating services come up short too often, producing marriages that lead too often to divorce. Now, with genetic testing, we know how to pair up people disposed to find each other permanently irresistible.

Use an *imagine what it would be like* opening

There is a dream, and you know how to make it into a reality. This variation on the new-opportunity idea would have worked well before mobile phones became ubiquitous:

> Imagine what it would be like if you could call anyone at anytime without finding a phone booth. Imagine what it would be like if you could call for help in the dark of night on a lonely road when your car breaks down. Imagine what it would be like if you could use the same device, fitting easily into your shirt pocket, to take notes, play music, and find a good restaurant. All that will soon shape all our lives, enabled by technologies now within sight.

Such an opening has several features: there is no jargon; there is no off-putting, elitist tone; and the picture painted invites interest from many kinds of readers.

Indicate *Steps*

You can build your *Steps* section easily around a list. The following appears in a paper on self-aware systems. The section title is *Steps: Building on the Genesis foundation*. I have just explained that a system built by Hiba Awad (2013) answers questions about stories involving cultural bias in attitudes toward violence, answering in particular the question, "Did Lu kill Shan because America is individualistic?"

> But while Awad's version of Genesis answered *yes*, it could not explain why it said *yes*. Getting Genesis to explain why was an obvious challenge, so we determined to take the following steps:
>
> • Work out an inner-language vocabulary of problem-solving actions.
> • Arrange for Genesis's problem-solving methods to tell a story in that vocabulary.
> • Have Genesis compose an elaboration graph using the inner story.

- Connect the inner-story elaboration graph to Genesis's externalization methods.

In this paper, we focus on the second step, that of arranging for Genesis's methods to tell a story. (Winston and Holmes, 2018)

Add *News*

News makes work current. Your paper is not about history, it is history being made. Select one of your Contributions that is both interesting and recent and make it News by putting a date on it. Write, "This past January, we showed how our results enable anyone to demonstrate cold fusion in their garage," or something like that.

What you need to know

Your writing is more likely to be read if you begin with essential *Vision*, *Steps*, and *News* elements:

- Start by stating your Vision. That is, identify a problem and indicate your approach to solving the problem.
- Express your Vision using a standard opening. Possible openings include the if-then, big-questions, interesting-story, mission-blocker, new-opportunity, and imagine-what-it-would-be-like openings.
- Demonstrate you are guided by a plan. Do so by indicating the Steps needed and identifying the step or steps you will discuss.
- Make your work current by identifying a major Contribution that has just happened. Provide a date. Make it News.

20 What to Put at the End

In this chapter, you learn what you should write about at the end of your written work. In particular, you learn the value of using a *Contributions* section, and you also learn some standard ways to express your Contributions inside your *Contributions* section. You can use these standard ways to ensure you finish with grace, much like the end-game strategies chess masters use to ensure a win.

Conclude with a *Contributions* section

Many authors seem unsure about how their written work should end. You see a menagerie of strange animal-in-the-headlights endings everywhere.

In written work, concluding with a *Contributions* section tells readers you have contributed something, and they will know you have contributed something when they are looking over your paper, deciding whether to read it.

As you learned in *Essentials of Persuasion* (page 7), habitually concluding with a *Contributions* section also forces you to think about what you have contributed.

Express your *Contributions* in an *enumeration*

You can express your Contributions as an enumeration of your Contributions much as you would on a *Contributions* slide. Then, add text that captures something like what you would say if you were to present such a slide, as in the following example:

For more on *Contributions* slide, see page 73.

> I have articulated principles of story summary and shown how those principles are reflected in the Genesis story summarizer. In particular, I have:
>
> • Argued that a reader model is a necessary foundation for a good story summary.

- Identified the principles of connection, concept focus, dominant concept focus, and interpretation transparency.
- Suggested *means* compression and introduced *post hoc ergo propter hoc* processing.
- Exhibited an implemented, principle-based summarizer at work on a representative story from the Genesis library, a précis of *Macbeth*, showing a compression of 84%. (Winston, 2015)

For more on especially appropriate verbs, see page 74.

Note the use of *argued*, *identified*, *suggested*, and *exhibited*, all of which are active, especially appropriate verbs.

Express your *Contributions* in a *bold statement*

Albert Einstein finished his paper on special relativity, *On the Electrodynamics of Moving Bodies*, with a summary statement of the Contribution:

> These three relationships are a complete expression for the laws according to which, by the theory here advanced, the electron must move. (Einstein, 1905)

The Einstein example, and the historical examples that follow, were not inside *Contributions* sections, but if they were, they would more immediately have been seen to be Contributions.

Express your *Contributions* as *good news*

For more on mission-blocker, see page 180.

If you use the mission-blocker opening, then you can pair it with a *good-news* Contribution:

> Thus, by arranging for intelligent systems to tell themselves the story of what they are doing, we ensure that they can explain what they are doing to us, mitigating the danger of harm from intelligent systems that do not know what they are doing. (Winston and Holmes, 2018)

Express your *Contributions* in *British understatement*

James Watson and Francis Crick finished their DNA paper, *A Structure for Deoxyribose Nucleic Acid*, with British understatement. The following is the effective ending, although at the very end, there is a short paragraph promising that more details will be published and a bit of acknowledgment.

> It has not escaped our notice that the specific pairing we have postulated immediately suggests a possible copying mechanism for the genetic material. (Watson and Crick, 1953)

Of course, this is just the clever way Watson and Crick chose to say: Yes, there is a Contribution here, we just figured out how Biology works.

Express your *Contributions* in a *grand insight*

Alan Turing finished his famous Turing-test paper, *Computing Machinery and Intelligence*, with grand insight:

> We can only see a short distance ahead, but we can see plenty there that needs to be done. (Turing, 1950)

Of course you can end just about any paper with what Turing wrote, so maybe it is an ending not so grand.

Express your *Contributions* in a *spreadsheet*

While just about everything you write should conclude with Contributions, *Contributions* is not the right title for every purpose. For example, if you are writing a business plan, you should conclude with how much money you expect to make, optimistically and pessimistically, in the form of a spreadsheet or equivalent graph or statement. Use a section title such as *Projected earnings*. After all, making money is the *sine qua non* of an investment.

Do not conclude with a *Conclusions* section

You could truthfully populate a section titled *Conclusions* in many ways. You could say: There is a lot of literature on the subject of my paper. The problems are hard. Other people approach the problems in other ways. There is much more to be done. Ice is cold.

Nobody will care. You need to conclude your paper with a *Contributions* section that forces you to write about what people do care about.

What you need to know

Your writing is more likely to be read if you end with a review of your Contributions:

- If you end with a section titled *Contributions*, you naturally have to think about what you have contributed and you tell your readers you have Contributions worth knowing about.

- The standard way of expressing Contributions is in a list, using appropriate verbs.

- Other ways of expressing Contributions include the use of a bold statement, a British understatement, a grand insight, a bit of good news, or in the case of a business plan, a spreadsheet or equivalent.

- Never conclude with a section titled *Conclusions*. What you have concluded may be of little interest because it is of little worth or has been concluded before; readers care about what you have contributed.

21 How to Write an Abstract

In this chapter, you learn that you should use a checklist when you write an abstract to ensure you have included all the *Vision*, *Steps*, *News*, and *Contributions* elements. You also learn that you should include details that make your Contributions tangible.

Use a VSN-C checklist

An abstract is a miniature paper serving two purposes: the self-serving purpose is that you want the larger story—your entire paper—to be read; the public-service purpose is that you do not want anyone to waste time poking around only to discover your paper is not for them.

Because an abstract is a miniature paper, most abstracts should have the usual VSN-C elements.

For more on VSN-C, see page 8.

There surely must be News, because if there is nothing new, then there is no paper. On the other hand, if the problem aspect of your Vision is well known to those for whom you are writing, you may limit the Vision statement to articulating your approach. You may not need to include Steps because they are implied by your Contributions.

Details sell

Restaurateurs appreciate the selling value of details. One of my students, Toan Tran-Phu, noted that you do not have much of an idea of what you will get if you order the following:

Salmon with vegetables

On the other hand, you can readily imagine what you will get, with a desired impact on your appetite and the restaurateur's profit, if you order this:

Saumon à la Crème de Poireaux et Champignons: At-
lantic salmon filet pan-roasted and topped with julienned
leeks and shiitake mushrooms in a savory garlic and shal-
lot cream sauce.

Readers are like restaurant customers. They need detail to decide if
they want what you have to offer. So put in details, with numbers.

Answer questions such as these: How long is your proof? How
many lemmas are there? How many neonate ferret brains did you
rewire? How long did it take those rewired ferrets to develop visual cells in their auditory cortex? How many training samples
did you provide to your learning program? How fast does it learn?
How accurate does it get? What kind of stories does your program
read? Which stories in particular? What kind of prior knowledge
did it have? How much?

Consider the following made-up example; it offers no details:

The NIMA system is based on recent advances in brain
function. It combines multiple agents to solve classic challenge problems in the literature. This paper describes the
overall architecture, explains how the parameters of the
architecture can be fine-tuned, and offers suggestions for
further work.

Where does the acronym come from? What advances? How recent? How many is multiple? Which classic problems? What literature? What kind of parameters? How many? Fine-tuned for
what? How many suggestions?

Note the contrast with the abstract of the paper that stimulated the
surge of interest in deep convolutional neural nets. That abstract
offers plenty of detail:

We trained a large, deep convolutional neural network
to classify the 1.2 million high-resolution images in the
ImageNet LSVRC-2010 contest into the 1000 different
classes. On the test data, we achieved top-1 and top-
5 error rates of 37.5% and 17.0% which is consider-
ably better than the previous state-of-the-art. The neural
network, which has 60 million parameters and 650,000
neurons, consists of five convolutional layers, some of
which are followed by max-pooling layers, and three

fully-connected layers with a final 1000-way softmax. To make training faster, we used non-saturating neurons and a very efficient GPU implementation of the convolution operation. To reduce overfitting in the fully-connected layers we employed a recently-developed regularization method called "dropout" that proved to be very effective. We also entered a variant of this model in the ILSVRC-2012 competition and achieved a winning top-5 test error rate of 15.3%, compared to 26.2% achieved by the second-best entry. (Krizhevsky et al., 2012)

From the abstract, I learned exactly what was achieved and the size of the system that achieved it. I read on. I excuse the authors for including two acronyms because they reasonably expect potential readers to know that GPU means Graphical Processing Unit and ILSVRC means Imagenet Large Scale Visual Recognition Challenge.

Write it, then rewrite it

Some years ago, my student Sajit Rao had a personal problem, so he rushed the writing of his PhD thesis (Rao, 1998) to meet a deadline. He handed a draft to me early on the due date. I gagged. The research work was terrific, but the abstract was not:

This thesis explains how visuospatial representations and processes can be used not only for recognizing objects and directing action but may also be reused for more abstract tasks such as understanding language or doing arithmetic. Several lines of evidence indicate that there may be no clear distinction between perception and "high-level" cognition. If we are to use this insight in our efforts to build a humanoid robot, then it is important to understand:

- What makes underlying perceptual machinery flexible enough to be re-used for inference?

- What is the representation(s) of the perceptual knowledge that may be the basis for understanding language and reasoning?

To this end, this thesis is focused on fleshing out a model of visual attention. We discuss how the model can:

- Extract a wide variety of spatial relations on demand.

- Learn visuospatial patterns of activity (visual routines) from experience.

I could not make out the Vision, Steps, News, and Contributions. The thesis explains, not the author. The royal *we* in *we discuss* shouts for attention. No details explain what could be done now that could not be done before. The abstract mentioned humanoid robots, but the thesis did not.

Rao sat down with me and went to work, rewriting it completely. I now use that experience as the basis for a classroom exercise.

First, my students and I get rid of the thesis-as-actor phrase. We also change the royal *we* to *I* and adjust some wording so that programs compute, not models:

This thesis In this thesis, I explain....
We I discuss how programs based on the model can....

Then, we strike out the part about humanoid robots, and we make the causal statement less tentative:

Because I believe there is no clear distinction between perception and "high-level" cognition, If we are to use this insight in our efforts to build a humanoid robot, then I think it important to understand:

With the deletion, there is no explanation of why Rao's work was important. There is no Vision. We start to replace the entire first paragraph:

If we are to develop a computational account of human intelligence, we have to develop an understanding of the problem-solving capability of the human visual system, because that system solves an amazing range of problems in the course of everyday activities.

The new if-then opening includes two instances of *we*, but these are not royal: they both refer to the community of researchers interested in developing a computational account of human intelligence, not the author.

Next, we stimulate interest with examples of the amazing range of problems solved by the human visual system:

> Without conscious effort, our visual system finds a place on the table to put down a cup, selects the shortest check-out queue in a grocery store, and looks for moving vehicles before we cross a road.

Then, we decide to make clear that Rao took two contribution-constituting Steps: Developing a theory of visual attention, and writing a program that extracts and learns:

> I have taken one step toward understanding the problem-solving capability of the human visual system by developing a theory of the visual attention subsystem. I have taken another step by writing, demonstrating, and experimenting with programs that extract a wide variety of spatial relations on demand and that learn patterns of attention shift from experience.

At this point, we strengthen the Contributions by adding a detail-providing explanation of just what sort of relations the program can extract:

> The extraction program finds a pointing relation between a pointing person and a large red cube. The program relies on primitive operations that establish low-level visual properties, such as feature size and orientation, at the focus of attention. The primitive operations constitute a powerful *language of attention*.

Next, we add detail that explains what the learning program actually learned:

> The learning program learns the pattern of visual activity evoked whenever a ball falls off a table. The program builds on the idea that notions such as *falling* can be

linked to patterns of attention shift. I show how my language of attention supports the extraction, from experience, of such patterns, ...

The clarifying detail paints a picture. Nothing like it had been done before. It is the News.

We decide we want to be sure those readers who know about Shimon Ullman's pioneering work on visual routines realize that this work by Rao builds on an idea Ullman proposed but had not implemented:

> .... and I explain that these learned patterns constitute *visual routines*, a kind of sequential visual program proposed by Shimon Ullman.

At this point, the abstract is better, but too long. Also, some journals limit abstracts to a single paragraph. We prune out the remarks about what the human vision system does, and we prune out the general statements about what the programs do in favor of the specific statements. All that can go into the introduction, so nothing cherished is lost completely.

The pruning leaves fewer than 120 words, about 56% fewer than before pruning:

> If we are to develop a computational account of human intelligence, we have to develop an understanding of the problem-solving capability of the human visual system. I have taken two steps toward that understanding: I developed a theory of visual attention, and I wrote, demonstrated, and experimented with programs based on that theory. A spatial-relation extraction program finds a pointing relation between a pointing person and a large red cube using primitives that shift attention, find features, and determine feature orientation. A learning program learns about falling by noting the pattern of visual attention activity evoked whenever a ball falls off a table. Such patterns constitute instances of Ullman's *visual routines*.

For more on Krizhevsky et al., see page 188.

One flaw remains. Conspicuously and in contrast to the Krizhevsky et al. abstract, Rao's abstract offers no evaluation numbers. His aim was to demonstrate capability for the first time, not to demonstrate capability better than others using some easy metric involving success rate on a standard data set.

Nevertheless, Rao's abstract would have been stronger had he told us something about how often his programs failed and under what circumstances. As is, we are left to decide for ourselves whether we are satisfied with an implied approach to evaluation that equates success with the demonstration of a program that at least sometimes recognizes pointing and learns to recognize falling.

Otherwise, the final result exhibits all the important elements. The Vision statement asserts that you have to understand the human visual system if you want to understand human intelligence. The Steps enumeration explains that Rao developed a theory, then implemented, demonstrated, and experimented with programs, all of which constitute Contributions. The citation indicates that Rao's work builds on Ullman's visual-routines proposal. Details tell us that the primitive operations shift attention, find features, and determine feature orientation, and that Rao's programs recognize pointing and learn about falling, providing some News.

Thus, readers of the revised abstract readily see the big problem that Rao addresses, the approach, the Steps, and the Contributions. Such readers know what they need to know to decide whether to read on.

Exploit your broken-glass outline

The Rao example starts with an abstract that needed much repair. What should you do if you start with a blank sheet of paper?

In *Essentials of Outlining* (page 29), you learned about broken-glass outlines. If you make one in preparation for writing, then the top-level spokes tell you how to focus your abstract and a few low-level spokes likely suggest details to include.

What you need to know

The abstract is the most important part of a paper because the abstract has a major effect on whether the rest is read. You should write it, rewrite it, get fresh eyes on it, and have it critiqued by someone who does not know what you do.

- You should be sure your abstract expresses your Vision, identifies the Steps you have taken, articulates some News, and lists your key Contributions.

- Your abstract should include detail that makes your Contributions tangible. In particular, your abstract is a good place to brag about your performance numbers.

- Once you have a broken-glass outline, you have a good start on abstract composition.

You can observe a lot by watching.

Commonly attributed to Yogi Berra; American professional baseball player, manager, and coach

22 How to Learn by Imitation

In this chapter, you learn that you can write better by imitating what you like and by reading well-written history and literature.

Learn from great writers

The first edition of James Watson's *Molecular Biology of the Gene* (Watson, 1965) impressed me beyond description.

When I thought about why the book impressed me, I noted several features:

- With the book open, you see one or two section headings. You always see a breaking point coming up where you can pause and reflect or go for coffee.

- The section headings consist of full sentences. They summarize content.

- Illustrations appear frequently, with highly instructive captions. They, too, summarize content.

Watson's style invites emulation.

Naturally, I incorporated these elements of Watson's style into my own writing.

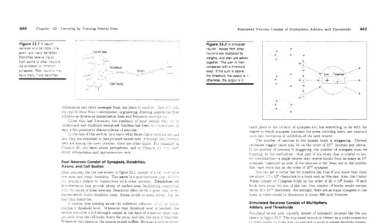

Back when I wrote a textbook on Artificial Intelligence, I made sure that full-sentence headings appear on almost every page, that illustrations appear on almost every page, and that each illustration carries a highly instructive caption. From Winston (1992).

Reading great writers
makes you a better writer

We humans are great mimics. If you read Shakespeare with a glass or two of wine, you will start speaking Elizabethan English. I have been known to talk about all those slings and arrows of academic politics.

If you read well-written literature or history, you will write better yourself, not as well as Shakespeare, but better than before.

Knowing of my interest in the American Civil War, my colleague Robert Berwick came into my office some years ago, handed me a book, and said, "You have to read this." It was James McPherson's *Battle Cry of Freedom*. "How did you like it?" Bob asked a few weeks later. "It was terrific!" I replied.

Then, he asked, "Do you know why it reads so well?" I admitted I did not. I felt it read well, but I had not thought to think why. Bob opened the book to a random page (page 460) and read this sample passage out loud:

> Jackson intended to overwhelm Shields's advance force and then face about to attack Fremont. But the stubborn resistance of Shields's two brigades at Port Republic frustrated the plan. Three thousand bluecoats held off for three hours the seven or eight thousand men that Jackson finally got into action. The weight of numbers eventually prevailed, but by then Jackson's army was too battered to carry out the attack against Fremont, who had remained quiescent during this bloody morning of June 9. Both sides pulled back and regrouped. That night Jackson withdrew to Brown's Gap in the Blue Ridge. (McPherson, 1988)

Why does it read so well? Because McPherson deploys active verbs. They paint pictures in your mind as you read.

> Jackson <u>intended</u> to overwhelm Shields's advance force and then <u>face about to attack</u> Fremont. But the stubborn resistance of Shields's two brigades at Port Republic <u>frustrated</u> the plan. Three thousand bluecoats <u>held off</u> for

three hours the seven or eight thousand men that Jackson finally got into action. The weight of numbers eventually prevailed, but by then Jackson's army was too battered to carry out the attack against Fremont, who had remained quiescent during this bloody morning of June 9. Both sides pulled back and regrouped. That night Jackson withdrew to Brown's Gap in the Blue Ridge.

The passage exhibits only one passive-indicating *was*. If McPherson wrote passively, you would see something like the following instead, with all the life sucked out of it by the substitution of nine passive *was* and *were* words for the active verbs:

Overwhelming Shields's advance force was intended by Jackson so that Fremont could be attacked by him. But the plan was frustrated by the stubborn resistance of two of Shields's brigades at Port Republic. The seven or eight thousand men that finally were gotten into action were held off by three thousand bluecoats for three hours. The weight of numbers eventually was the prevailing factor, but by then Jackson's army was so battered that an attack against Fremont, who was quiescent during this bloody morning of June 9, was not carried out. Both sides were pulled back and were regrouped. That night Jackson's army was withdrawn to Brown's Gap in the Blue Ridge.

When you write this way, you too easily eliminate the actors who perform the actions by deletion of the *by* phrases, as in the following version of the first three sentences:

Overwhelming Shields's advance force was intended so that Fremont could be attacked. But the plan was frustrated. The seven or eight thousand men that finally were got into action were held off.

Engineering and science literature is often full of sentences that have the look and feel of equations. Variations on the *is* verb are abundant. Sentences are lifeless and dull. The work is good but the writing is not.

Hmmm. That paragraph reads better this way: Engineering and science literature, by contrast, often includes an abundance of equations that masquerade as sentences. Authors destroy their writing with variations on the *is* verb. Sentences bore and exhibit no life. The work excites, but the writing sedates.

Assemble your own examples of great writing

You may think a work is great because of the way the author deploys verbs. You may like an author's preference for short, Anglo-Saxon words. You may like the author's way of mixing short and long sentences.

For more on voice, see page 3.

Reserve a special shelf for such work in your library. Pick out a random piece from time to time and read from it, noting why you think it good. Then, your own writing will become more like that. The genre does not matter as long as you admire the voice.

What you need to know

To be a better writer, you should read and admire good work, both technical and nontechnical.

- Ask why you like what you like, then imitate what you like.
- Read well-written history or literature that features verbs that evoke images.
- Look for sentences in which you can replace *is* with an active verb.
- Assemble a library of writing you admire; reread samples as a writing warm-up exercise.

If you have any young friends who aspire to become writers, the second-greatest favor you can do them is to present them with copies of The Elements of Style. *The first-greatest, of course, is to shoot them now, while they're happy.*

Dorothy Parker; American poet, writer, and critic

From "The Elements of Style Turns 50," by Sam Roberts in the *New York Times* (Roberts, 22 April 2009)

23 How to Avoid Style Blunders

In this chapter, you learn to recognize and avoid errors typically committed by writers who have never had their work reviewed by a talented editor with a red pencil, liberally deployed.

Read classic works

When I was working on the draft of my first textbook, I showed it to a Wellesley student, who happened to be taking my Artificial Intelligence subject at MIT. "What do you think?" I asked. I got the much dreaded reply:

"Have you read Strunk and White?"

She was asking, of course, if I had read *The Elements of Style*.

I had read it, but I had not studied it. I have studied it many times since. Critics say the book is not consistent and that it violates many of its own rules. To them I repeat Emerson's famous maxim: "A foolish consistency is the hobgoblin of little minds" (Emerson, 1979).

Read Strunk and White's *Elements of Style* (2014).

Then, just as I was finishing my third or fourth book, my editor at Addison-Wesley asked me if I had a preference for a copy editor. At this point, I thought I knew everything any copy editor could tell me, so I said, "Find someone who can make me cry." He replied, "Oh, I'll see if Lyn Dupré has some time." She did, and I almost did, hammered as I was by mistakes that you can read about in *BUGS in Writing*. And she is a developmental editor, not a copy editor, because she also makes structural suggestions.

Read Dupré's *BUGS in Writing* (1998).

While you wait for your copies of *Elements* and *BUGS* to arrive, read on. I explain the errors you should fix first because they are the errors that identify you as especially uninterested in what your readers think of your writing.

Honor essential elements of grammar and style

Grammar and style errors mark you as careless or inexperienced or both. Many readers will be unforgiving, especially those, like me, who have been beaten up by knowledgeable professional editors. Do not spoil your good work; be careful and honor the essentials.

Use *I*, not *we*, if you are the sole author

We means the author and the reader or the authors. Unless you are a king or queen, or you are one of multiple authors, do not use *we* when you are referring to yourself as the author. Someone, somewhere, decided it was egotistic to use *I*, but the *we* convention can lead to confusion about who is actually responsible for the work.

Note the first sentence in Alan Turing's famous paper *Computing Machinery and Intelligence*:

> I propose to consider the question, "Can machines think?" (Turing, 1950)

Thus, if you use *I* in your papers, you are in good company.

When you write documentation, however, you should use *we*, because you write as a surrogate for your organization:

> We suggest that you back up your work frequently.

> We recommend that you encrypt your password file.

Do not write as if your paper is a living person

You explain your work in your paper; your paper itself lacks sentience and has no capacity to think:

Anthropomorphic:	This paper explains desktop cold fusion.
You do it:	In this paper, I explain desktop cold fusion.

I spent a few minutes in DSpace, MIT's online research archive, and sadly turned up many examples like these in thesis abstracts:

Bad: This thesis seeks to test the effects....

This thesis will describe the experimental....

This thesis will explore....

This thesis argues....

This thesis discusses....

This thesis analyzes the limitations of ....

This thesis explores the underlying principles....

Strangely, I also discovered that MIT evidently exhibits astonishing admissions bias toward royalty. Nearly all the theses I examined, all written by a single person, used the royal *we* pronoun rather than *I*.

I found a few heartening exceptions. Evidently, ordinary people wrote some of the theses, and they worked without the aid of the thesis itself:

Good: In this thesis, I describe...

In this thesis, I explain....

In this thesis, I propose....

Do not use *previous, former,* and *latter*

Previous, former, and *latter* force your reader to stop reading, to scan back, and to reread previous material. Use an unambiguous reference instead:

Bad: I like sports, especially the sport I discussed previously.

Good: I like sports, especially skiing.

Bad: I like skiing and hiking. I like the former because....

Good: I like skiing and hiking. I like skiing because....

Do not use *above* and *below*

When you refer to another place in your writing, use the most precise pointer possible:

Often vague: I could have committed the *below* blunder above.

More precise: I could have committed the *below* blunder in the first sentence of this section.

When referring to figures, use figure numbers if you allow your document-processing software to move your figures around. Otherwise a figure you refer to as the figure below may turn out to be above or not the next figure shown.

Do not use *since* when you mean *because*

Because means that there is a causal connection. *Since* means that time has passed. Using *since* to mean *because* is inelegant:

Wrong choice: He took 6.034 since it is a great course.

Correct choice: He took 6.034 because it is a great course.

Ambiguous: He has taken gut courses since he decided to go to law school.

Unambiguous: He has taken gut courses because he decided to go to law school.

Unambiguous: He has taken gut courses since the day he decided to go to law school.

Strangely, Strunk and White do not adhere to this rule. They often use *since* when they mean *because*.

Do not use *last* when you mean *past*

Last means last. You have not experienced the last year, last month, last week, or last day, unless the end of the world is imminent. *Past* means the most recent:

Pessimist: During the last year, we made spectacular progress. Too bad, because there will be no more years.

Optimist: During the past year, we made spectacular progress. Great news, because we will be able to build on that spectacular progress in the coming year.

Do not utilize *utilize*

The devil made me write *utilize*. A good test is that if *use* works, then *use* is the right choice:

Bad: They utilize the best equipment money can buy.

Good: They use the best equipment money can buy.

Do not use *thing*

Thing is the ultimate abstraction. Use a more precise word:

Avoid: His writings include things that drive me crazy.

Better: His writings include grammatical mistakes that drive me crazy.

Do not use pronouns

Each of us has only one language processor, from which the following principle emerges:

For more on language processor, see page 83.

Minimization principle: Write to minimize your reader's unnecessary linguistic computations so your reader's language processor can focus on your ideas, not on your syntax.

One kind of unnecessary linguistic computation is that required whenever a pronoun appears. Generally you should just repeat the noun to which the pronoun refers.

Marvin Minsky joked that stories written for children were often harder for computers to understand than news accounts. Consider the following children's story about a birthday party:

> Peter and Paul were going to John's birthday party. One of them wanted to buy a kite. "But he has one," he said, "he will make you return it."

Lacking common sense, computers stumble over all the pronouns:

> Peter and Paul were going to John's birthday party. <u>One</u> of <u>them</u> wanted to buy a kite. "But <u>he</u> has <u>one</u>," <u>he</u> said, "<u>he</u> will make <u>you</u> return <u>it</u>."

Unlike writers of stories for children, journalists avoid pronouns, preferring less ambiguous anaphoras, as in this exaggerated news account:

> Peter recently announced an intention to buy a kite for John because the young man's birthday party is imminent. A reliable source disclosed that Paul criticized the proposed purchase. "John has a kite," Paul said to Peter, "John will make you return your gift to the store."

Using the *reliable source* phrase, the journalist tells you the journalist will not identify the actual source.

If your first language happens to be a language such as German or Russian, you should be especially careful with pronouns. In those languages, gender helps to resolve pronoun references, so you can get away with a usage habit that does not work well in English.

Do not call a shovel a spade

Many authors somehow think it is bad to repeat a word, so if they have been using a word such as *shovel*, they switch gratuitously to *spade*, leaving their unfortunate readers wondering whether the switch indicates a deliberate meaning shift or a careless inconsistency or a silly desire to avoid repetition.

> His bloated presentation consisted of 85 <u>slides</u>. Each of the <u>projections</u> had too many words. All those <u>PowerPoints</u> put me fast asleep.

Respect the difference between *that* and *which*

That introduces phrases that help to disambiguate referents. Do not use *that* if the referent is already unambiguous; use *which* instead. *Which* adds information. Do not use *which* to introduce a phrase that is helping to disambiguate a referent.

Disambiguating:	Patrick lives on Creepy Street in the house *that* has a white Volvo parked in the driveway.
Adds information:	Patrick lives on Creepy Street in the last house on the left, *which* has a white Volvo parked in the driveway.

In the vernacular of grammarians, *that* introduces restrictive clauses, and *which*, non-restrictive clauses.

Never write or say *try and*

Amazingly, even professional newscasters, on nationally broadcast programs, occasionally say *try and*: "The President said he would *try and speak* to the nation on the subject." They should replace *try and* with *try to*: "The President said he would *try to speak* to the nation on the subject."

Horrible:	He decided to try and study all night.
Correct:	He decided to try to study all night.

Use quote marks only when you are quoting someone

Do not use quote marks to suggest that a word is misused. You can write about so-called deep neural nets, but should not write about "deep neural nets." If you use quotes, some readers will think you have a limited vocabulary or could not remember the appropriate word.

Tell your story yourself

Your reader wants to learn about your idea, not those of a quoted person. The role of a quoted person is to buttress your idea, not express it.

Quote co-opts your story:	Winston has "worked on AI research as a way to understand human intelligence for many years."
Quote supports your conclusion:	Winston is committed to research aimed at understanding human intelligence: "I've worked on AI research as a way to understand human intelligence for many years."

Never use apostrophes to make acronyms or time periods plural

One personal computer is a PC. Many are PCs, not PC's. The first great work in Artificial Intelligence was done in the 1960s, not in the 1960's.

Eliminate the inessential

Ernest Hemingway, a great novelist, short-story writer, and journalist, is noted for his simple, lean, concise style of writing. Some say his style could be traced to when he worked as a European correspondent for the *Toronto Star* newspaper in the 1920s; communication was by cable and words were expensive.

Aspire to simple, lean, and concise. Be like Hemingway. Eliminate inessential words, phrases, sentences, and paragraphs.

Scan for bugs

Whenever I write a book, including this one, I do a find-replace, after everything else is done, to replace all misused *which* instances. Many authors and editors refer to this process as the *which hunt*.

I also look at instances of *since*, because maybe they should be *because*. I search for instances of *thing*, *utilize*, *former*, and *latter* that I can purge. I find passive verbs and replace them with active verbs.

Get the help you need

If you are not a native speaker of the language in which you are writing, seek help from friends, institutional resources, or a professional copy editor.

When only maximal effort is good enough, hire a developmental editor to examine your thesis or book or other great opus. Such editors not only find spelling and grammatical errors, they offer structural advice.

What you need to know

If you write carelessly, you will irritate many readers and make your ideas harder to understand. Accordingly, you should allocate time for writing improvement:

- Read classic works on writing. Read Strunk and White (2014); read Dupré (1998).
- Use *I* not *we*.
- Do not write as if your paper were its own author.
- Do not use *former* and *latter*.
- Do not use *above* and *below*.
- Do not use *since* when you mean *because*.
- Do not use *last* when you mean *past*.
- Do not use *utilize* when you mean *use*.
- Do not use *thing* when you can use a more specific word.
- Do not use pronouns.
- Do not switch words gratuitously.
- Do not use *which* when you mean *that*.
- Do not try and do anything; try to do it.

- Do not use quotes to convey your idea; use quotes to support your idea.
- Do not use quotes unless quoting someone.
- Do not use apostrophes to make acronyms or time periods plural.
- Eliminate inessential words.
- Do a final scan for misused words.

Where you can learn more

For more instruction on writing, see *The Elements of Style* (Strunk and White, 2014) and *BUGS in Writing* (Dupré, 1998). You may also benefit from *Do I Make Myself Clear?: Why Writing Well Matters* (Evans, 2017), a book that argues, at considerable length, for brevity.

I hate writing, I love having written.

Commonly attributed to Dorothy Parker; American poet, writer, and critic

24 How to Defeat Writer's Block

In this chapter, you learn what to do when you know you want to write, but you cannot get started.

You are not alone

When I thought this book was finished, I found myself exchanging emails with the acquisition editor at Addison-Wesley I worked with back when I wrote textbooks. Over the course of our email chitchat, he wrote:

> One of these days I'll develop sufficient discipline to sit still and finish my own book, decades in the making; I have used up every excuse I learned over many years in publishing, and no longer have even a virtual dog to eat the manuscript.

He was suffering from writer's block, a name for that kind of inhibition that prevents a writer from writing. I concluded there was one more chapter that had to be written, this one. It took a while because I had a hard time getting started on it.

You have many options

Many writers experience writer's block, so if you experience it, you are neither weird nor alone.

Some people have writer's block because they have not fully crystallized what they want to say; others because they have yet to fit writing into their daily routine; still others because they feel overwhelmed by the enormity of the effort.

Fortunately, there are many options for confronting various forms of writer's block. One of them or some combination of them may work for you.

Ease into what you want to say

Many fiction authors start by writing up detailed sketches of the characters who will populate a story. Then, they drop the characters into interesting situations, at which point the story almost writes itself. Some do not know how their stories will end when they start to write.

Similarly, you should not think you have to finish your work before you start to write about it. New ideas emerge as you work up an outline, do a presentation, develop examples, and actually write because the writing process stimulates thinking.

Make a broken-glass outline

For more on broken-glass outlines, see page 30.

Your first task should be to make a broken-glass outline. I like to work at a blackboard, photographing with my mobile phone what I have when I like it. No one else sees what I do at this stage, so I experience no fear of ridicule.

Constructing a broken-glass outline on a blackboard enables me to add spokes easily and to subtract spokes with a swipe of my hand.

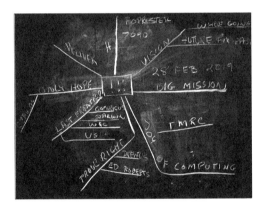

For more on analogs of broken-glass outlining for creative brainstorming, see page 34.

Constructing a broken-glass outline forces thinking about what you want to write. You ask yourself: "What is my vision?" "What examples should I use?" "For whom am I writing?"

If you cannot construct at least a rough outline, you may not have anything yet to say. When you have an outline in hand, you are almost done.

Schedule a presentation

Samuel Johnson always seemed to know how to say it. When a friend, William Dodd, an Anglican clergyman, was about to be hanged for various crimes, Johnson defended Dodd's authorship of a farewell sermon, remarking, "Depend upon it Sir, when a man knows he is to be hanged in a fortnight, it concentrates his mind wonderfully" (Womersley, 2008).

Johnson's remark invites paraphrase, this one for example: When you are scheduled to give a talk in the morning, it concentrates the mind wonderfully.

What do you do? You quickly make yourself a broken-glass outline; you use it to guide selections from your slide library and perhaps compose some new slides. Behold, you have started writing, hardly realizing that you have accomplished a lot.

Give the presentation. Then, to generate a written version, move text into annotating legends, leaving the pictures and diagrams in the slides. Next, add what you said when you gave the talk to the annotating legends. Preface the annotated slides with a VSN-C executive summary. You are almost done; all you need do is translate your annotated slides into text and figures.

For more on VSN-C, see page 8.

Explain it to a friend

If there is no venue for a presentation in sight, you can present to a friend, with or without slides, depending on what you are writing. You can record and transcribe what you say, using the transcription as a starting point.

If you use an imaginary friend, you are dictating, an approach that works well for some authors. Winston Churchill prepared his mammoth six-volume *The Second World War* (Churchill, 1948 to 1953), and many other books, via dictation followed by heavy editing of printed page proofs.

Write about the examples

If you are writing technical material, populate your broken-glass outline with examples featuring illustrations. Much of what you write will be explaining the examples and discussing the illustrations.

Just write, you can fix it later

A long time ago, before everyone had a computer, typewriters blocked writers, especially perfectionists. When you made mistakes, your pages looked like garbage dumps. You had to cut up pages, tape together sentences and paragraphs, and eventually type everything over, with fresh mistakes.

In those days, you conditioned yourself to edit in your head before typing. Words trickled out or stopped flowing altogether.

With computers, you are more likely to write fluidly and conversationally, knowing you can fix all your mistakes later. Passive sentences will be activated along with all the other defects and mistakes identified in *How to Avoid Style Blunders* (page 203).

Try freewriting

Even though you likely write with a computer, you may have conditioned yourself to edit in your head, giving yourself a habit you need to correct.

Noting the problem in himself, Peter Elbow, a Professor of Writing, recommends the practice of freewriting for 10 or 15 minutes a day (Elbow, 1998). Just write without stopping, without editing, without attention to grammar, knowing that you will not show what you write to anyone. And if you must, just write *stuck*, or *I have nothing else to write*, over and over. Just make it flow.

Eventually, some of what you write in your freewriting exercise will be worth saving, but the point is to learn to postpone editing until you have words in front of you.

Keep a notebook

Because an idea may emerge at an unanticipated moment, only to be lost in the next moment, many writers keep a notebook handy all the time. The notebook is there when an accidental happening leads to an epiphany. It is there in the middle of the night when a big idea emerges in a dream.

Into the notebook, day and night, go clever ways of expressing thoughts, breakthrough approaches to tough problems, and ideas for new projects.

Condition yourself to write

Like Pavlov's dogs conditioned to salivate at the sound of a bell, we, too, can be conditioned. In particular, we can condition ourselves to write.

Reserve time just for writing

Some part-time authors get to work early, before others show up, and write in that quiet time before distractions intrude. Some devote Saturday morning to writing. In the end, regularity is what matters.

Make a space just for writing

Some authors work in a home office. Some work in a shed. I wrote most of the first edition of *Artificial Intelligence* (Winston, 1977) in a local cafe, surrounded by noise that somehow masked itself. A colleague of mine, with class notes and detailed outline in hand, retreated to a hotel room for a week to finish a book.

You want a special place to write, in part, because you need to separate yourself from routine distractions. You want physical or psychological barriers to temptation emerging from access to media, social media, family and friends, and people dropping by.

You also want a special place to write because going to that place becomes part of your writing ritual.

Take a walk, go jogging, promise yourself a break

Sometimes, when you get stuck, you just need a thinking break. Sometimes when I am stuck, I go for a think-it-over walk. Sometimes a jog is better because jogging releases mood-improving endorphins.

Sometimes, when your determination wanes, you need to promise yourself a break. Just one more paragraph, and I will go putter in my woodshop for a while. Finish this section, and I will go plant some seeds. Draw this illustration, and I will stop to make coffee. Whatever it takes.

Sleep on it

Sleep is a kind of break. I am not sure if I make progress when I am actually sleeping, but when I get stuck, I sometimes take a nap, knowing that while sleep is coming, I am thinking about how to get unstuck.

Overcome fear

To me, writing feels creative, much like painting a picture. Before I learned to think about writing that way, writing was something I needed courage to do. If you need courage, you may benefit from advice from Ivan Sutherland.

Sutherland, noted for his pioneering work in computer graphics, wrote that he sometimes thought of himself as a kind of computer, executing a simple procedure, whenever he knows he needs to do something, but cannot work up the courage to do it. He explains via a story about washing dishes:

> I used to hate washing dishes. I would delay as long as possible. Eyeing the daunting pile of dishes, I would say to myself, "I'll be here forever." The enormity of the task deterred me from starting. But I now get the dishes done promptly because I learned a simple procedure for doing the job from my wife's uncle. The procedure starts out "Wash first dish...." (Sutherland, 1991)

By analogy, a writing procedure is: Write first sentence, or first paragraph, or if you are thinking of writing a three-volume biography of Winston Churchill, write first chapter.

What you need to know

- Get started by working up an outline.
- Force progress by scheduling a presentation.
- Explain your examples, and describe your illustrations.
- Write with abandon, you can fix everything later, once you have a draft.

- Keep a notebook; record ideas when you encounter them.
- Reserve a special time for writing.
- Reserve a special space for writing.
- Take a walk, go jogging, or promise yourself some kind of treat.
- Sleep on it, working your problem as you drift off.
- Drive out fear by focusing on a small initial step.

Part V
Design

Beauty will result from the form and correspondence of the whole, with respect to the several parts, of the parts with regard to each other, and of these again to the whole; that the structure may appear an entire and complete body, wherein each member agrees with the other, and all necessary to compose what you intend to form.

Andrea Palladio; 16th-century Venetian architect

From *The Four Books of Architecture (Dover Architecture Book 1)* (Palladio, 1965) Chapter 1, page 1

25 How to Make Design Choices

In this chapter, you learn why you should know the basics of good design even if you work with a professional graphic designer.

Design matters

You need the right design, just as you need the right words, to ensure that your communications are clear, easy to follow, and memorable. With good design, your slides, posters, papers, proposals, books, and other materials look professional. With bad design, you encumber all the effort you put into what you say and write.

Someone may make your choices for you

If you are in government or work for a corporation, you may not have much say in the design of your communications. Your principal form of presentation is a slide presentation, and for the slides, your organization probably requires you to use a standard organization-specific theme.

Communication is Important

Symbols provide handles
Slogans provide handles
Salient ideas stick out
Surprises aid memory
Stories stimulate interest

The theme used by Ascent Technology, a company that offers powerful resource-allocation software. Ascent theme courtesy of Ascent Technology.

If you are an academic, you may not think much about overall design. For your publications, the publishing journal tells you how your written work must look. For your presentation slides, you may dream up something simple on your own or pick some sort of theme from your software's theme library.

The keep-it-simple principle usually rules out library choices, such as the theme on the right from Microsoft PowerPoint.

If you choose to use a library theme, do not pick a theme like the one on the right; that theme forces text to be in upper case in a bold, cramped, hard-to-read type family.

For more on type families, see page 235.

Many design choices remain

Even with the overall look determined, there is still a great deal of design work to do, probably by you. You need to arrange text, graphs, drawings, and pictures. You need to make choices about how your graphs present quantitative information. You have to crop pictures. You have to choose a type family.

You want to do this design work carefully because you want the great ideas in your presentation to appear in nice clothes, not dressed in rags.

Stay in charge

You may work, by command or by choice, with a graphic designer who will arrange design elements, construct graphs, crop pictures, and choose a type family.

Big companies have entire departments full of graphic designers employed to construct slide packages. Those graphic designers may surprise you with what they do. In a slide presentation, each slide may have a mood-establishing picture. Text may be tilted.

Artistic innovation may distract attention from your Vision, Steps, News, and Contributions.

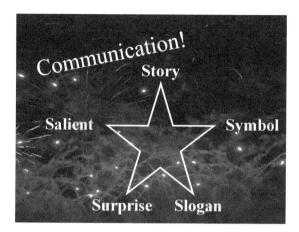

Designers like what they make, and what they make are works of art.

Good graphic designers are wonderfully talented, but remember that they are artists. Unless they have read this book, they do not know about the VSN-C idea. It is up to you to ensure that their designs support your ideas, rather than get in the way.

For more on VSN-C, see page 8.

Edward Tufte has harsh words for graphic designers who let art get in the way, especially for those who produce statistical graphics:

> Illustrators too often see their work as an exclusively artistic enterprise—the words "creative," "concept," and "style" combine regularly in all possible permutations,.... Those who get ahead are those that beautify data, never mind statistical integrity. (Tufte, 2001), page 79

And more generally, when making a presentation slide look good, one designer may make it so abstract, it has no message. Another may include chintzy clip art, making your slides look goofy to many audiences. Still another may insist on using a type family that has artistic qualities, even though it is difficult to read. So listen and admire, but do not abdicate your authority as the communicator.

What you need to know

You need to know the basics of good design because how your work looks influences how people respond to your work.

- Even if your organization decides how your communication looks and feels, you still have many design decisions to make as you arrange design elements, construct graphs, crop pictures, and choose a type family.

- Even if you work with a professional graphic designer, you need to know enough about design to be sure proposed designs will work with your ideas and will look right to your listeners and readers.

26 How to Arrange Graphics

In this chapter, you learn how to arrange graphical elements using a layout approach based on placing graphical elements in a grid.

Use the grid layout scheme

Students of graphic design learn about an idea developed in Switzerland in the late 1940s (Müller-Brockman, 2017). They learn that arrangements of graphs, drawings, pictures, and text generally look better when aligned using a grid of equally sized rectangles separated by corridors. This grid has four rows and three columns:

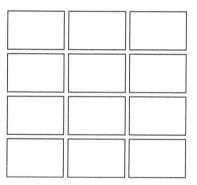

A basic grid consists of rectangular areas arranged in rows and columns with spaces in between.

After you decide on your grid dimensions, you place your elements in individual rectangles or in rectangular combinations.

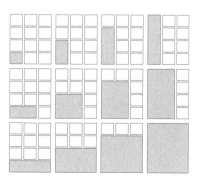

A 4×3 grid offers 12 rectangle size choices.

An 8×6 grid offers 48 rectangle size choices, three of which are shown.

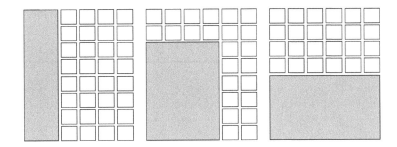

Grid layout turns a sow's ear into a silk purse

To see how the grid idea helps transform a slide, consider the following mixture of text and pictures of various sizes, some overlapping, arranged to illustrate poor design. The images are provided by Ian Tattersall, who is noted for simple, often text-free slides.

⊘ The words are superfluous; the design hopeless. It is a sow's ear. Images courtesy of Ian Tattersall.

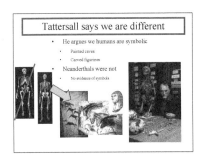

I got rid of the title and text because I will say what is written anyway.

⊘ The layout remains ugly beyond description. Images courtesy of Ian Tattersall.

Next, I rearranged the layout, resizing and aligning the pictures.

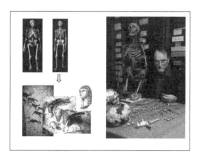

⊘ The layout remains ugly, but not beyond description. Images courtesy of Ian Tattersall.

Then, after some experiments, a 2×4 grid emerged as my choice for moving the pictures into a grid.

I decided to use a grid layout, 2×4.

Finally, I cropped and scaled the pictures to fit, rearranging them in accordance with what I had to say.

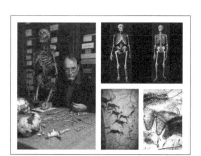

It looks much better, more like a silk purse. Images courtesy of Ian Tattersall.

No text is required when developing a slide for oral presentation. If not for presentation, then text would be required, which may conveniently fit in the corridors between rectangles. Here is the general idea.

The corridors between rectangles offer convenient places for captions.

And here is the idea specialized to the example.

The corridors between rectangles offer convenient places for captions. Images courtesy of Ian Tattersall.

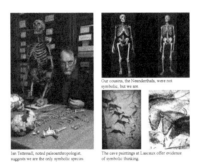

Note how the hierarchy of ideas emerges as you scan left-to-right, top-to-bottom: Tattersall tells us we are special; that flows into special relative to Neanderthals; and that flows into just how we are superior.

Grids also work with text elements

Architects of various sorts use grids on poster-sized plans and in proposal books. Here is a proposal by a landscape architect for reviving Revere Beach in Revere, MA.

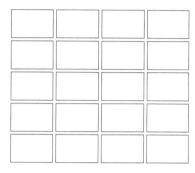

After some thought and experiment, the landscape architect chose a 5×4 grid.

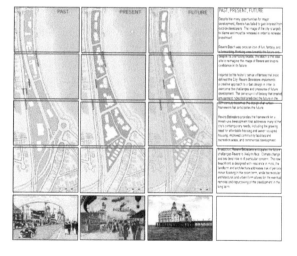

Next, she fit maps, pictures, and text into the grid, with some cropping. Image courtesy of Sarah Winston.

Finally, she removed the grid lines. Image courtesy of Sarah Winston.

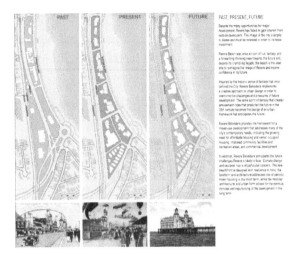

Once again the hierarchy of ideas emerges.

What you need to know

Habitual use of a grid system will not qualify you as a graphic designer, but it will improve the look of your presentations.

- When you arrange graphs, drawings, pictures, and text, use a grid system.
- When you use a grid system, you place graphs, drawings, pictures, and text into the rectangles in a grid or in rectangular combinations of those rectangles.

Where you can learn more

You can learn more about the grid system from Josef Müller-Brockman's book *Grid systems in graphic design*, which also has a brief but interesting discussion of type families (Müller-Brockman, 2017).

To learn more about Ian Tattersall's research into how we acquired symbolic thinking, see *Becoming Human* (Tattersall, 1998), *Human Evolution and Cognition* (Tattersall, 2010), *Masters of the Planet: the Search for our Human Origins* (Tattersall, 2012), and *At the Birth of Language* (Tattersall, 2016).

27 How to Select Type Families

In this chapter, you learn the vocabulary of type, which includes terms such as *type family*, *typeface*, *font*, *glyph*, *serif*, and *ligature*. You also learn the pros and cons of various type-family choices.

Understand type families, typefaces, and fonts

A *type family* is a set of related *typefaces*. Times, Computer Modern, Georgia, Garamond, Sabon, and Helvetica are type families. Regular, bold, and italic are typefaces. A *font* is a typeface in a particular size.

You measure size in points

In the vernacular of typography, an ascender is the part of a character that lies above the mean line, which you can think of as sitting on the top of an *x*. In the Sabon typeface, which I use in this book, the letters b, d, f, h, k, and l have ascenders that reach to the highest level. A descender is the part that lies below the baseline, which you can think of as located at the bottom of an *x*. The letters g, j, q, p, and y have descenders.

A *point* equals 1/72 inch or 0.0353 centimeter. Twelve points equals a *pica*. The size of a font is a little more than the distance from the top of the ascenders to the bottom of the descenders.

The little-more qualification dates back to when type was set with individual blocks of lead, each of which had a block height large enough to contain the largest characters with a little space above the ascenders and below the descenders. Consequently, when you measure a font, it may be surprisingly smaller than the lengths of the ascenders and descenders suggest. To get the exact size you want generally requires some experimenting.

Insist on ligatures in your type family

When a character is printed on paper or displayed in a screen, what you see is called a *glyph*. Better document-preparation systems, such as LaTeX, provide special glyphs for character combinations that would look ugly if rendered by their individual glyphs. Consider the *fi* and *fl* combinations, for example, as rendered in an ordinary word processor:

fine flags

The *fi* and *fl* combinations look awkward. But when rendered with *ligatures*, glyphs that artistically combine the *f* with the *i* and the *f* with the *l*, you see this:

fine flags

Use serif type families in written work

A *serif type family*, like the one used for the body text in this book, features characters that have supplemental decorations at the end of the strokes. A *sans serif type family* does not. Here are examples of a serif type family and a sans serif type family:

Times is a serif type family. Boxes surround the serifs.

Helvetica is a widely used, sans serif type family.

Helvetica

Should you use a serif type family or one without serifs? Curiously, all the books in my library that are written by graphic designers, and none otherwise, are set in sans serif type families. Typically, graphic designers say sans serif type families look cleaner and more modern.

Edward Tufte, in *The Visual Display of Quantitative Information*, disagrees, quoting Josef Albers:

> The fashionable preference for sans-serif in text shows neither historical nor practical competence.
> (Tufte, 2001), page 183

I agree with Tufte and Albers, so I limit my use of sans serif type families to headings. I acknowledge that the question of legibility remains controversial.

I also acknowledge that most serif type families do not work well on low-resolution devices such as older mobile phones. Text written for such devices should be in a sans serif type family or in a serif type family, such as Georgia, designed specifically for low-resolution devices.

Know the characteristics of the standard type families

I am not fussy about choosing type families for slides; generally I just use whatever version of the standard Times family happens to be available. There should not be so many words on a slide, or at such a small size, that readability is an issue.

On the other hand, I am fussy about type families for books, and a little fussy about type families used in papers.

Whenever I write a book, I consult a book designer who will offer suggestions about type-family selection. Then, I set a few pages in the suggested type family to see how it feels to read text in the suggested type family, with emphasis on *read*.

The following samples show the look of several popular type families. Note the differences in the space occupied and the relative lightness and darkness of the characters. The sample paragraph comes from the Foreword (pp. ix–x) of Julia Child's *Mastering the Art of French Cooking* (Child et al., 1971).

Helvetica

An extremely popular sans serif type family, designed by Max Miedinger in 1957, widely used in signage and books on graphic design. Sample requires nine lines.

Our years of teaching cookery have impressed upon us the fact that all too often a debutant cook will start in enthusiastically on a new dish without ever reading the recipe. Suddenly an ingredient, or a process, or a time sequence will turn up, and there is astonishment, frustration, and even disaster. We therefore urge you, however much you have cooked, always to read the recipe, even if the dish is familiar to you. Visualize each step so you will know exactly what techniques, ingredients, time, and equipment are required and you will encounter no surprises.

Times

A compact, widely acceptable type family, designed in 1931 for *The Times* (London) newspaper, with a view toward maximizing the number of words printable on a page. Sample requires eight lines.

Our years of teaching cookery have impressed upon us the fact that all too often a debutant cook will start in enthusiastically on a new dish without ever reading the recipe. Suddenly an ingredient, or a process, or a time sequence will turn up, and there is astonishment, frustration, and even disaster. We therefore urge you, however much you have cooked, always to read the recipe, even if the dish is familiar to you. Visualize each step so you will know exactly what techniques, ingredients, time, and equipment are required and you will encounter no surprises.

Computer Modern

The default type family for users of LaTeX; good for documents with mathematics. Keeps the number of words on a page low, so you feel like you are getting somewhere as you read. Sample requires nine lines.

Our years of teaching cookery have impressed upon us the fact that all too often a debutant cook will start in enthusiastically on a new dish without ever reading the recipe. Suddenly an ingredient, or a process, or a time sequence will turn up, and there is astonishment, frustration, and even disaster. We therefore urge you, however much you have cooked, always to read the recipe, even if the dish is familiar to you. Visualize each step so you will know exactly what techniques, ingredients, time, and equipment are required and you will encounter no surprises.

Georgia

Our years of teaching cookery have impressed upon us the fact that all too often a debutant cook will start in enthusiastically on a new dish without ever reading the recipe. Suddenly an ingredient, or a process, or a time sequence will turn up, and there is astonishment, frustration, and even disaster. We therefore urge you, however much you have cooked, always to read the recipe, even if the dish is familiar to you. Visualize each step so you will know exactly what techniques, ingredients, time, and equipment are required and you will encounter no surprises.

A type family designed for use with low-resolution computer and device screens, designed by Matthew Carter in 1993. Sample requires nine lines.

Garamond

Our years of teaching cookery have impressed upon us the fact that all too often a debutant cook will start in enthusiastically on a new dish without ever reading the recipe. Suddenly an ingredient, or a process, or a time sequence will turn up, and there is astonishment, frustration, and even disaster. We therefore urge you, however much you have cooked, always to read the recipe, even if the dish is familiar to you. Visualize each step so you will know exactly what techniques, ingredients, time, and equipment are required and you will encounter no surprises.

A venerable, often used type family, originally designed by Claude Garamond in 1535. Sample requires ten lines.

Granjon

Our years of teaching cookery have impressed upon us the fact that all too often a debutant cook will start in enthusiastically on a new dish without ever reading the recipe. Suddenly an ingredient, or a process, or a time sequence will turn up, and there is astonishment, frustration, and even disaster. We therefore urge you, however much you have cooked, always to read the recipe, even if the dish is familiar to you. Visualize each step so you will know exactly what techniques, ingredients, time, and equipment are required and you will encounter no surprises.

A type family based on Garamond, designed by George W. Jones in the late 1920s. Named for Robert Granjon, a 16th-century type cutter and printer. Sample requires ten lines.

239

Sabon

Another type family based on Garamond, designed by Jan Tschichold in 1960s. I use Sabon in this book and in several textbooks. Sample requires nine lines.

Our years of teaching cookery have impressed upon us the fact that all too often a debutant cook will start in enthusiastically on a new dish without ever reading the recipe. Suddenly an ingredient, or a process, or a time sequence will turn up, and there is astonishment, frustration, and even disaster. We therefore urge you, however much you have cooked, always to read the recipe, even if the dish is familiar to you. Visualize each step so you will know exactly what techniques, ingredients, time, and equipment are required and you will encounter no surprises.

Large sizes reveal differences

Many type families are so similar you need to see them in a large, 50-point size to see the differences:

Garamond

abc...lmn...xyz

Granjon

abc...lmn...xyz

Sabon

abc...lmn...xyz

The differences are even easier to see in the 80-point versions of the Garamond, Granjon, and Sabon z:

zzz

Julia Child used Granjon

Evidently, Child—or her designer—was fussy about the type family used in *Mastering the Art of French Cooking* (Child et al., 1971). The following is from the book's colophon, set, of course, in Granjon:

> This type face [Granjon] was designed by George W. Jones, who based his drawings on a type used by Claude Garamond (1510–61) in his beautiful French books, and more closely resembles Garamond's own than do any of the various modern types that bear his name.

Granjon is the right type family for a book about French cooking. The type-family choice, along with other aspects of the book design, supports the content in a way other type families could not. Like the recipes described, Granjon is classic and subtle.

Choose from a few standard type families

Unless you are a type-family aficionado, you should stick with a few conservatively selected type families. I usually use Sabon for text and Frutiger or Helvetica for headings. If I am composing text that involves a lot of mathematics, I use Computer Modern. If I am composing text for low-resolution electronic devices, I use Georgia. For slides, I use the default type family or Times.

Ignore Latin text samples when selecting type families

Sometimes type-family samples show up in the form of a scrambled excerpt from a Latin text by Cicero, starting with *Lorem ipsum dolor*.... Unless you are writing in Latin, make no judgment based on such a sample. You want to know how a type family reads and fits your communication, not how it looks in a language you do not understand.

What you need to know

You have many type options for your slides, posters, papers, proposals, books, and other materials. To make an informed choice, you need to know the vocabulary with which people discuss, admire, and condemn the options.

- Regular, bold, and italic are typefaces.
- A type family is a set of typefaces with common features.
- Type size is given in points. A point equals 1/72 of an inch; a pica equals 12 points.
- Serifs are decorations at the end of character strokes. Ligatures are glyphs that replace character combinations that otherwise look awkward when juxtaposed.
- Type aficionados argue about whether serif or sans serif type families are more readable. On slides, there should be so few words and the size should be so large that readability is not an issue with any of the popular choices.
- Graphic designers like to use sans serif type families in their books because they like the clean, modern look. This book uses a serif type family for the text because many people believe text in a serif type family is easier to read.
- When you write for small-screen devices, use a type family designed for small screens.

Where you can learn more

If type fascinates you, you can learn much of all there is to know from Emil Ruder's *Typographie* (Ruder, 1967).

You cannot count yourself as a real type aficionado unless you have seen *Helvetica*, the documentary film directed and produced by Gary Hustwit, released in 2007 on the 50th anniversary of the Helvetica type family's introduction. I have friends who claim they have watched it multiple times.

The interior decoration of graphics generates a lot of ink that does not tell the viewer anything new. The purpose of decoration varies—to make the graphic appear more scientific and precise, to enliven the display, to give the designer an opportunity to exercise artistic skills. Regardless of its cause, it is all non-data-ink or redundant data-ink, and it is often chartjunk.

Edward Tufte; American statistician, educator, and author

From *The Visual Display of Quantitative Information* (Tufte, 2001), page 107

28 How to Work with Graphs

In this chapter, you learn a few principles for displaying quantitative information in slides, posters, papers, proposals, books, and other materials. Those basic principles will help you to ensure that your displays will be properly understood and tell no lies.

Get rid of chart junk; keep it simple

Document preparation systems enable you to *"decorate"* words in all sorts of ways—you can change size, use color, use italic, underline, and put in quotes, but that does not mean you ever should.

Similarly, you can use all sorts of tricks when you display quantitative data—you can use pictures of coins instead of simple bars when displaying financial information. You can ask your graphing software to switch to a 3D look. You can use unneeded legends. You can shrink the axes. Edward Tufte, author of the definitive book, *The Visual Display of Quantitative Information* (2001), calls the results of such design manipulations *chart junk*. Here is an example.

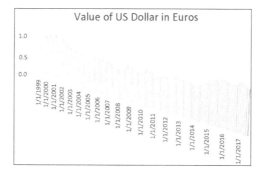

⊘ An exchange-rate graph showing, in three dimensions, how many euros you could buy for a US dollar between 1999 and 2017. This particular graph is shaded and given a three-dimensional look.

Just because you can do such tricks with your graphing system does not mean you should. Tricks get in the way of communication, just as when you decorate a word with useless features.

Get rid of the shading and the three-dimensional look.

Another version of the exchange-rate graph, this one without shading, without the mean-ingless three-dimen-sional look, and with larger fonts.

Tell the truth; do not squander clarity to save space

Whenever space is limited, you may be tempted to shrink the range of the vertical axis and use a small font. Here, the exchange rate range has been reduced; it is no longer 0–1.4; it is 0.6–1.2.

⊘ Another version of the exchange-rate graph with a nar-rowed vertical axis.

Narrowing the range on the vertical axis tells a lie. Our eyes are powerful problem solvers, and they, contradicting what you see when you look at the numbers, suggest that the maximum to min-imum ratio is about ten times larger than it really is.

You have saved about one-third of the space occupied, but for-feited truth, because your eyes suggest to you that the maximum is about 20 times the minimum, rather than just under two times the minimum. You have to look carefully at the numbers on the vertical axis to understand what really happened.

Misleading graphics are easy to find

Even reputable publications publish graphics that mislead your eyes. An issue of a consumer magazine, which I skimmed through while taking a break from writing this chapter, reported on when it was best to buy various appliances, concluding that early November is good.

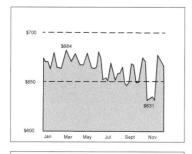
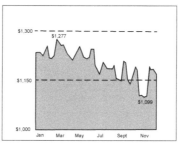
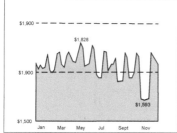
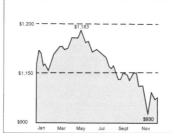

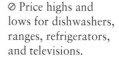

⊘ Price highs and lows for dishwashers, ranges, refrigerators, and televisions.

All the graphs have the same height, presumably to provide a pleasing, uniform look. Unfortunately, with shrunken vertical axes, the graphs mislead your eyes. Ignoring the high and low numbers, just looking at the graph, it looks like you pay, at the yearly low, 63% less for a dishwasher and a whopping 90% less for a television. You actually pay 8% less for a dishwasher and 21% less for a television.

Use labels, not keys

Now suppose you want to graph the exchange rate of the GBP and the euro in US dollars. Your graphing system may propose to use a key so you can see which is which.

⊘ An exchange-rate graph showing how many euros and GBPs you could buy for a US dollar between 1999 and 2017. This particular graph uses a key to indicate which line goes with euros and which line goes with GBPs.

Your graphing system does what it can, but does not realize that when you use a key, your reader's attention has to move back and forth between the key and the graph, noting what each color means while looking at the key, then look for the corresponding colors, expending mental effort. You should instead use labels; they require no big movement of the eyes, no shift in attention, and no thinking about which color goes with which currency.

This exchange-rate graph uses labels, rather than a key, to indicate which line goes with euros and which line goes with GBPs.

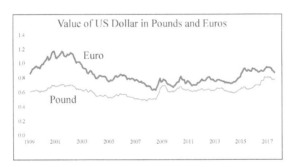

What you need to know

Our eyes are magnificent problem solvers; that is why graphs are almost always better at conveying quantitative information than tables. Unfortunately, there are many ways bad practices mislead our eyes. A few simple rules will keep you away from the most grotesque of the bad practices commonly seen in the display of quantitative information.

- Get rid of chart junk. Just because you can use chart junk does not mean you should.

- Tell the truth. Space-saving needs or graphic design inspiration must not lead to portrayals that mislead eyes.

- Use labels. Avoid keys.

- Use a precise, explanatory title.

Where you can learn more

To learn more about the visual display of quantitative information, see *The Visual Display of Quantitative Information, second edition* (Tufte, 2001).

Those who want to be serious photographers, you're really going to have to edit your work. You're going to have to understand what you're doing. You're going to have to not just shoot, shoot, shoot. To stop and look at your work is the most important thing you can do.

Annie Leibovitz; American photographer

From an interview by Rae Ann Fera in *Fast Company* (Fera, 28 June 2013)

29 How to Work with Images

In this chapter, you learn basic principles for working with images in slides, posters, papers, proposals, books, and other materials.

Crop images using the rule of thirds

Many professional photographers move the most important element of an image away from the center. Asked to explain why, they offer all sorts of exotic explanations, but you do not have to believe any of the explanations to benefit from the practice.

Consider, for example, the following images of Andrea Palladio's Chiesa del Santissimo Redentore, commonly known as Il Redentore, in Venice, Italy. In one image, the church is in the center, boringly; in the other, off center, interestingly.

Il Redentore, designed by the 16th-century Venetian architect, Andrea Palladio; built to celebrate deliverance from the bubonic plague of 1575–1577.

How far off center should you put the important element? Authors of books on photography often advise using the rule of thirds: divide the image space into thirds with horizontal and vertical lines and put the most important element of the image at one of the places where the lines intersect.

For the image of Il Redentore, the rule of thirds dictates the following placement as one of four possible places.

Il Redentore, appearing in the image according to the rule of thirds.

In the example, the horizon rests near one of the horizontal lines involved in the rule of thirds. In general, such placement of a horizon works well.

Use big images

Academic presentations tend to use design themes with titles.

Il Redentore, a slide element, along with a title.

Slide sets prepared by graphic designers generally omit the title and cover the entire slide with an image.

Il Redentore filling the entire slide.

Placing the most important element off center often leaves a place for a title. Many slide sets prepared by graphic designers consist entirely of slides such as the following in which the image covers the whole slide with an embedded title.

Il Redentore filling the entire slide, with an embedded title.

Which is better, the academic style or the graphic-designer style? For this question, neither answer stands as universally better. Be guided by community expectations and your own voice.

For more on own voice, see page 3.

Emphasize size with even bigger images

Graphic designers often arrange for images to extend beyond the sides of a slide to emphasize size. Such images are said to bleed off the sides.

Il Redentore extends beyond the top and right of the slide, emphasizing size.

Aspect-ratio preferences evoke controversy

The aspect ratio of an image is the ratio of the length of the long side to that of the short side. If an image fills a slide produced by a standard slide-preparation system, that software likely offers aspect ratios of 4:3 or 16:9, which are ways of saying 4 parts width to 3 parts height, or 16 parts width to 9 parts height, or ratios of $4/3 \approx 1.33$ and $16/9 \approx 1.78$.

The standard aspect ratios offered by commonly used slide-making software.

The aspect ratios offered by commonly used slide-making software match the 4:3 ratio of television sets initially sold in the United States and the 16:9 ratio of the newer HDTV television standard.

For more on grid layout, see page 229. If your images are embedded in a grid layout, your aspect ratio may be fixed by your choice of grid dimensions.

Otherwise, you probably should use an aspect ratio greater than 1:1 and less than 2:1. Few will criticize your choice if it is between 4:3 and 5:3, which are, as decimal numbers, about 1.33 and 1.67.

The golden rectangle emerges from mathematical constraint

Artists of various kinds have argued about the right aspect-ratio choice for millennia, with many looking to mathematics or music for esthetic guidance. Those looking to mathematics tend to like an aspect ratio of about 1.62, the aspect ratio of the *golden rectangle*.

Here is how you make a golden rectangle: start with a square; then, add a rectangle as in the following.

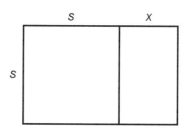

A golden rectangle.

The resulting rectangle is golden if the ratio of the long side to the short side of the outer rectangle is the same as the ratio of the long side to the short side of the inner rectangle:

$$\frac{s+x}{s} = \frac{s}{x}$$

From this equality of ratios, you have:

$$x^2 + sx - s^2 = 0$$

Then, putting the quadratic formula to use, you have:

$$x = \frac{-s + \sqrt{s^2 + 4s^2}}{2} = \frac{-1 + \sqrt{5}}{2}s \approx 0.62s$$

Thus, the width to height ratio of a golden rectangle is about 1.62. So is the width to height ratio of the embedded rectangle, so the embedded rectangle is a golden rectangle, too, which means it too consists of a square plus a golden rectangle, and that pattern continues without limit.

Some claim the facade of the Parthenon forms a golden rectangle, but it may be that the architects simply chose the proportions because they thought the building would look good, which it did and does.

The Parthenon may have been designed with the golden rectangle in mind. Adapted from image by Eusebius (Guillaume Piolle) via Gnu Free Documentation License.

Musical consonance suggests ratios of integers

Other architects found inspiration in music. Palladio, known for building not only churches but also villas, favored floor plans in which the rooms are either circles or rectangles, the dimensions of which form ratios considered consonant by musicians.

If the frequency ratio of two notes is 1:1, you have what musicians call a perfect first; 4:3 is a perfect fourth; 3:2 is a perfect fifth; 5:3 is a major sixth; and 2:1 is an octave.

Six of Palladio's favorite ratios. All but the $\sqrt{2} : 1$ ratio are considered consonant by musicians.

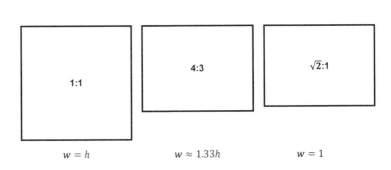

1:1   4:3 $\sqrt{2}$:1

$w = h$ $w \approx 1.33h$ $w = 1$

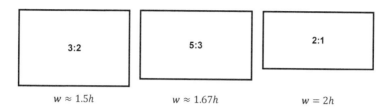

The aspect ratio of the golden rectangle is close to that of a 5:3 rectangle, differing by only 3%:

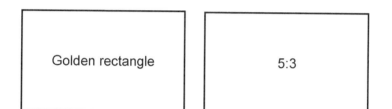

The golden rectangle's aspect ratio, ≈ 1.62, is close to 5:3, ≈ 1.67.

What you need to know

Great photographers are skilled artists. Your photographs will look more like those of great photographers if you follow a few rules:

- Use the rule of thirds. That is, place what you want viewers to focus on at one of the four intersections where horizontal and vertical lines divide your image into thirds.
- Whenever your images include the horizon, put the horizon one third up or two thirds up from the bottom.
- Experiment with images that fill the entire slide.
- Use proportions, such as that of the golden rectangle, considered pleasing to the eye.

Part VI
Special Cases

Take away that pudding—it has no theme.

Commonly attributed to Winston S. Churchill; British statesman, writer, and Prime Minister

Remark to a waiter, often used by Patrick Henry Winston as a metaphor when reacting to a poster

30 How to Prepare a Poster

In this chapter, you learn how to prepare a poster, sometimes called a board, so that it attracts attention and promotes engagement.

Posters need an element that pops

All kinds of meetings include poster sessions, from science fairs to research conferences. Topics include not only science and engineering, but also myriad other foci, from start-up ideas to theological scholarship. Designers use them to show off their work at design competitions. Developers use them to promote ideas for urban design projects. Posters are everywhere.

Wondering whether my poster-viewing habits are peculiar, I surveyed a dozen colleagues who attend poster sessions. All reported that they stop at only a fraction of the posters, and those posters all have one characteristic in common: something pops.

I first learned the meaning of *pop* in a meeting with people at Addison-Wesley, discussing the design of one of my books. They did not care much about the interior design or even the cover design; they cared a lot about the color of the spine. Red, I learned, is good. In a bookstore, the books with red spines tend to stand out, or *pop* in the vernacular. Your eyes are drawn to them. I insist that my books have red spines.

So what can pop in a poster? What is the analog of a book spine? One possibility is the title; another is a graphical element.

But neither is enough; the title or graphical element just gets you over the first hurdle. Then, you need something else that draws a potential viewer further in.

Posters need an element that expresses *Contributions*

To get over the next hurdle, you need a *Contributions* element in your poster.

Once, I walked through a poster room populated by approximately 100 graduate students and postdoctoral researchers preparing themselves for the job market. My time was limited, so I decided I would stop only at posters that not only popped, but also displayed conspicuously articulated research contributions. I did not stop.

I am sure beyond doubt that many of the posters described work that would interest me, but if I could not be sure of that at a glance, I just kept going. I did not want to get stuck and waste a presenter's time.

For more on *Contributions* sections, see page 11. If any poster had a *Contributions* section, or at least a title that described a Contribution, I would have been drawn into a discussion, possibly making useful suggestions, possibly recommending the work to a colleague, and perhaps making a difference.

Posters invite artistic design

In presentations, you are the star and your slides are supporting elements. In a poster session, your poster takes on a more central role, and you become the commentator.

For more on VSN-C, see page 8. Thus, you can exercise more artistic license with a poster than with rapidly traversed slides. You just need to be sure that your graphic artistry highlights, rather than obscures, your VSN-C story.

You can use an augmented VSN-C structure

Robert McIntyre's poster on brain preservation has conspicuous *Vision* and *Steps* sections that populate the left column, with *News* and *Contributions* sections that populate the right column.

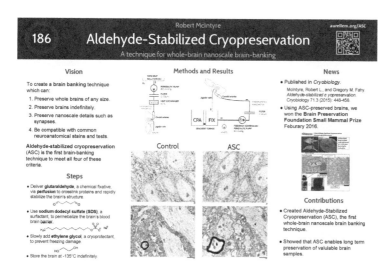

Poster by Robert McIntyre. Note the VSN-C structure. Image courtesy of Robert McIntyre.

Shakespeare pointed out that a rose by any other name would smell as sweet. So you need lose no sleep if community expectations require you to do some label substitutions as long as you retain the sense of VSN-C.

Oscar Rosello included no explicit *Steps* section and no explicit *News* section, but the *Contributions* section reflects steps and all the pictures describe an experiment just completed.

This poster by Oscar Rosello has no Steps and no News, but the big picture pops, and there are conspicuous *Vision* and *Contributions* elements in the column under the title. Image courtesy of Oscar Rosello.

Sometimes circumstances—supervisor demands, field traditions—require posters to have particular elements. Nicole Seo had to include explicit *Previous work*, *Research question*, *References*, and *Acknowledgments* in her poster. Here is how she included all these while still retaining a VSN-C structure.

Poster by Nicole Seo. Note the VSN-C structure. Image courtesy of Nicole Seo.

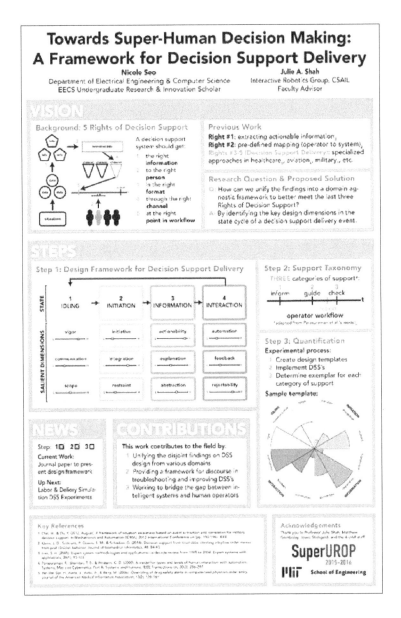

You can capture everything in a storyboard structure

When you are standing at a poster, presenting what you have done, you are telling a story. So you may reasonably choose to organize your poster in a way reminiscent of what filmmakers call a *storyboard*. A storyboard is a kind of visual plan consisting of a series of graphical elements, each accompanied by a caption describing what will go on at the corresponding point in the film.

In a filmmaker's storyboard, the graphical elements stand in for fragments of a film. In a poster, the graphical elements may be much like the slides that would appear in a slide show: some may be pictures or graphs; others may carry questions, statements, or terse, carefully crafted bullet lists.

When a poster is in storyboard form, it works well whether or not you are there. If you are present, you point at the graphical elements, thus encouraging your listeners to ignore the captions. If you are somewhere else, then the captions say what you would have said.

You can start with a grid layout like the following for a poster developed for explaining how to design posters. The *Vision*, *Steps*, and *News* elements all occupy up-front positions; the final position is labeled *Contributions*. Together the four elements tell each passerby that you have an idea, you have a plan, something cool has just happened, and you have contributed.

For more on grid layout, see page 229.

The structure of a storyboard poster. Four elements, *Vision*, *Steps*, *News*, and *Contributions*, open and close your story.

The *Vision* element, closer up, has a caption meant to be read only if you are not present. Otherwise, you encourage your audience to ignore them by pointing at where you want them to focus.

Josh Haimson deployed the storyboard structure in the following poster. Most of the text lies in captions, to be read only when Haimson was absent.

Poster by Josh Haimson. Note the storyboard character. He uses a grid layout, but includes the captions in the grid rectangles instead of in the corridors. Image courtesy of Josh Haimson.

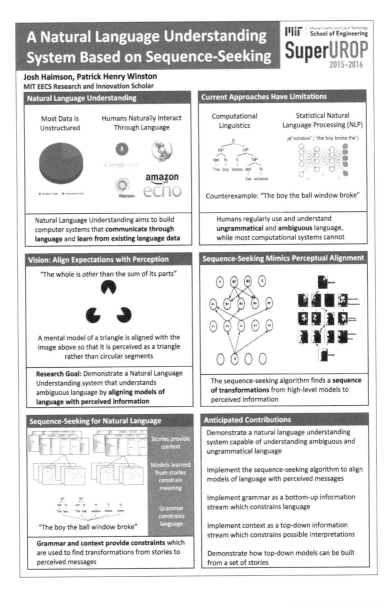

Electronic posters offer advantages and disadvantages

Many poster sessions now feature large screens instead of places to attach paper posters. You can make last-second changes; you need not find a place that prints posters; you can include video.

Unfortunately, you also can replace your everything-in-one-place poster with a story distributed over two or many slides. While you are talking with someone over a final slide, those walking by do not stop and join in because they see no Vision; while you are waiting for someone to become interested, no one becomes interested because they see no Contributions. Multiple middle slides ensure that those eager to work the whole room become impatient and discourage others from stopping.

You can benefit from the advantages and avoid the disadvantages if you limit yourself to one or two slides. If you use more than one slide, include the *Vision* and *Contributions* elements in each.

A quad chart is a poster on a slide

Directors of research organizations that fund dozens of projects often learn about those projects from program managers who prepare briefings with one slide for each of the contributing organizations. Each slide is much like a poster because the slide summarizes a lot of effort in one visual display. And each slide has all information arranged in four prescribed quadrants to ensure that no time is spent during the briefing on deciphering structure.

A standard quad chart has a title along with quadrants for a picture and phrase, impact, new ideas, and milestones.

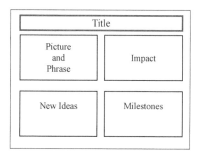

Quad charts are concise summaries.

You may never prepare a quad chart, but it is still useful to see what quad charts contain, because quad charts, like posters, constitute effective summaries of proposed work. Many proposal writers compose quad charts for their own eyes only, as a first step in proposal writing, to ensure that their proposals feature elements they know program managers will want to see.

Typically, the *Impact*, *New Ideas*, and *Milestones* quadrants consist of bullet lists, with three to five items each. Those, together with the *Picture and Phrase* quadrant, collectively capture the essence of a project.

For more on Symbol, Slogan, Salient idea, and Surprise, see page 21.

Sometimes, the in-charge person insists on a *bumper sticker*, a term of art meaning a phrase that summarizes the summary, often highlighted in yellow. A bumper sticker is a good place to put a Symbol, Slogan, Salient idea, or Surprise.

Some quad charts include take-away content in a bumper sticker.

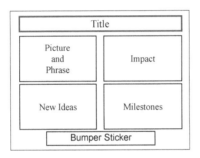

For more on VSN-C, see page 8.

The various parts of a quad chart correspond to aspects of the VSN-C structure augmented by various elements drawn from *Essentials for Being Remembered* (page 15)

The *Picture and Phrase* quadrant provides handles

The *Picture and Phrase* quadrant corresponds roughly to Slogan and Symbol, two of the elements that make content more memorable. They serve as handles for the work you are describing, and they could introduce the problem part of your Vision and supply a bit of News.

The *Impact* quadrant exposes tailored Contributions

The *Impact* quadrant corresponds to the Contributions part of VSN-C. The *Impact* quadrant may also include a Surprise.

When preparing the *Impact* quadrant, you must focus on what the sponsor cares about. If you are writing for a science-oriented sponsor, your Contributions address scientific problems. If you are writing for a military-oriented sponsor, your Contributions address problems that prevent someone from accomplishing their mission.

The *New Ideas* quadrant explains your unique Vision

The *New Ideas* quadrant focuses on the approach part of your Vision. The *New Ideas* quadrant may also contain a Salient idea.

The *Milestones* quadrant promises specific Steps

The *Milestones* quadrant corresponds to the Steps part of VSN-C. You write the *Milestones* section carefully because each item promises something. By such and such a date you obligate yourself to do something definite—to develop, implement, demonstrate, evaluate,....

For more on Steps, see page 69.

For more on something definite, see page 74.

Never use *improve* or any synonym of *improve*. If you do, you will come off as a mere incrementalist, making tiny advances, not as someone who takes technology to another level.

Be specific, so as to give yourself room for a bigger promise next time around. This is too general:

- 1 January: Demonstrate a deep neural net trained using images drawn from various sources.

This is better:

- 1 January: Demonstrate a 25-layer deep neural net trained using 10 million images of 1,000 types of animals drawn from the World Wide Web.

What you need to know

To be noted, posters, also known as boards, require careful thought about layout and content.

- Having an element that pops characterizes the most successful posters.
- Each poster should have a *Contributions* section. For ongoing work, the section may be titled *Anticipated Contributions*.
- Each poster should have not only a *Contributions* section at the end, but also *Vision*, *Steps*, and *News* sections at the beginning. That is, posters are like any other kind of persuasion-oriented communication.
- If your poster might be viewed when you are absent, you should consider a storyboard format, with captions that fill in for you when you are somewhere else.
- A quad chart is much like a poster; a quad chart summarizes a great deal of work in a single visual.
- Typical quad charts have quadrants for a picture and phrase, impact, new ideas, and milestones. In these quadrants, you express your Vision, Steps, News, and proposed Contributions as well as a Symbol, Slogan, Salient idea, and Surprise.
- Milestones are promises; be specific; supply dates and numbers.
- Milestones should never include words that suggest incremental progress. *Improve* is an incremental-progress word.

31 How to Give an Elevator Pitch

In this chapter, you learn about elevator pitches. The idea is that you find yourself in an elevator with someone you want to impress, perhaps a venture capitalist. You have the elevator ride, and only the elevator ride, to persuade that person to be interested in you and your idea.

Elevator pitches are not only for elevators

You should have an elevator pitch for everything you do. You are not likely to need it in an elevator, but at some point, maybe at somebody's soirée, someone will say, "What do you do?" If you haven't thought how to express what you do simply and in a few sentences, you will come across as an incoherent nut or worse.

VSN-C works

An elevator pitch expresses your Vision, Steps, News, and Contributions in a few carefully thought-out VSN-C sentences. A few extreme examples follow, with one sentence for each element. The first is an elevator pitch that Wilbur Wright and Orville Wright might have prepared following their first powered airplane flight in 1903. It uses an imagine-what-it-would-be-like Vision; the Contribution is business oriented:

For more on VSN-C, see page 8.

> **Start-up:** Imagine what it would be like to have flying machines deliver mail, perform reconnaissance, and even transport people. To make all that possible, we learned everything there was to know, and then we flew man-carrying kites, built lift-testing machines, and innovated. We just flew one of our machines 852 feet. Now we have a serious business opportunity because we hold key patents.

The next three elevator pitches are contemporary. The first two use an if-then Vision statement. The Academic example's Contribution is a new scientific understanding; the Defense example's Contribution is a way to overcome a mission blocker; and the Start-up example's Contribution is a game-changing business opportunity:

> **Academic:** If programs are going to be smart in the way we are, they will have to understand stories because story understanding is what makes us smart. We developed a theory of human story-processing and used it to write programs that summarize, persuade, and teach. One program has started to tell itself its own story, thus exhibiting an aspect of self-awareness. Soon all kinds of programs will explain what they are doing to themselves and teach themselves to do more.

> **Defense:** If we are going to accomplish our mission, we must reduce the cost of new weapons systems. In particular, we have to determine which emerging technologies can have the greatest impact, adapt them to mission needs, and get them into action with all possible speed. Emerging approaches to modeling and simulation offer great promise. Exploiting those new approaches will ensure our ability to defend against emerging threats.

> **Start-up:** We see tremendous opportunity for tutoring dolls that act like the pedagogues of ancient Greece. We are working through a technical development plan and a series of marketing steps aimed at getting the dolls into the hands of one-year-old kids who will learn from them everything from reading to the joys of scientific discovery. We just finished an exciting set of five prototypes that not only talk to the kids, but also collaborate with each other to solve behavior problems. A lot of people in Silicon Valley think this is going to be hotter than iPhone and Facebook put together.

Each contains about 100 words and takes about 20 seconds to recite. Unless you really are in an elevator, you are not likely to have so little time, but you should prepare an elevator pitch anyway. It is easy to expand from 20 seconds to a few minutes extemporaneously, but it is next to impossible to compress a 30- to 60-minute slide show into less than a minute without thinking it through in advance.

Even if you are sure you will never deliver an elevator pitch, you should prepare one. The preparation exercise forces you to know what your Vision looks like when reduced to its essence.

What you need to know

You should always have an elevator pitch ready for everything that you do; otherwise you may squander a big, but unanticipated opportunity. Elevator pitches are easy to compose in quiet, reflective moments, but impossible to compose spontaneously in elevators.

- Build your elevator pitch on a VSN-C foundation.
- Aim for 100 words or fewer.

I'm always nervous. I was nervous interviewing Malala and her father. It's an adrenalin thing, until the interview starts. Then you think: "Ok, I'm in the zone."

Christiane Amanpour; British-Iranian journalist and television host

Response when asked if she gets nervous before an interview. From an interview by Celia Walden in *The Telegraph* (Walden, 20 October 2013)

32 How to Be Interviewed

In this chapter, you learn how to prepare to be interviewed, and you learn how to minimize fear. You learn what you will be asked when you interview for undergraduate admissions, graduate admissions, and various kinds of job interviews. You also learn how to drive out fear in media interviews.

Anticipate questions

In many interviews, you can anticipate most of what you will be asked. Think about what you would ask if you were on the other side.

When one of my graduate students, Mark Finlayson, was preparing for faculty-job interviews, we knew he would be asked questions aimed at exploring how his work would contribute to the reputation of the university that hired him. We spent half an hour thinking what he might be asked.

Of the two dozen questions we anticipated, he was asked the following questions, variously expressed, more than ten times at each university he visited:

- Why is what you do important?
- With whom do you see yourself collaborating?
- Why do you want to join our faculty?
- How has the day been going?

All the questions, other than, "Why is what you do important," explore whether the candidate considers the host institution to be more than just a safety net.

We failed to anticipate just one important question, similarly targeted: What questions do you have for us? At first we thought the questioner was just being lazy, but then it occurred to us that questions like that are aimed at shedding light on whether a candidate has bothered to learn something about the interviewer's institution and its people. If not, neglect shows and offends.

A corollary comes to mind: if you are writing someone about becoming an intern, a graduate student, or a postdoctoral researcher, you better show that you know what that person actually does. Broadcast inquiries do not work.

Questions vary with the opportunity

If you are interviewing for undergraduate admission, your interviewer will want to know how you have handled a difficult situation, what you have done outside of school and school clubs, and how you will help in forming a balanced class. If you are interviewing for graduate school, your interviewer will be interested in what you can contribute to an ongoing research group.

If you are interviewing for your first industry job, the interviewer will explore your preparation for what the proposed job involves.

If you are interviewing for a new job of a kind similar to your previous job, the interviewer will want to know what you have accomplished and how. You may be asked:

- What do you like least about your current job?

A former student of mine likes to ask that question. There is no point in hiring someone to do something they do not like to do.

- Why do you want to work for us?

Another former student asks that question because he wants to know if the candidate really wants to work for Google and his company is the safety net. He wants to be sure his place is considered by the candidate as a first-tier choice.

In each case, you need to anticipate the questions and prepare truthful answers.

Work with your friends

Your best source of interview questions are friends who have recently been through the experience for which you are preparing. Talk to them. Make a list of the questions your friends have been asked, and think about how you might answer them.

Those same friends can also help you anticipate and prepare for interviewer styles. Some interviewers behave rudely to see how you handle difficult people. Some will take you to dinner to see if you drink too much alcohol or carelessly salt your food before you taste it. Some will want to know what you read or do for fun or whom you consider a hero. Make a list. Then, have friends interview you using your prepared lists.

Know what can happen in a media interview

The first time you are asked to do one, you may fear that you will be overcome with fear. I had that fear when Dan Rather, the anchor of the CBS Evening News for 24 years, came to interview me about Artificial Intelligence. It seemed like a big deal, so we touched up the paint in my office, and I dressed up a bit.

When the day came, my office started filling up with people. There were people with big bright lights, people with microphones, and people with wire-controlling gaffer's tape. There were people from the MIT News Office. There were people from the local CBS affiliate. Everyone wanted to meet Rather.

Before long I was immobilized in my desk chair by one of the people with microphones. The lights were bright. Everyone was talking to someone, except no one was talking with me. "How," I thought, "am I going to get through this?"

Then, Rather came in and sat down beside me. He started asking questions about my day, about MIT, about being a professor, all at such a low volume that all the fuss in my office seemed to retreat into the background. Then, when it was time to start recording, there was no break, he just started talking at a normal volume. There was no gap time. There was no time to get nervous. The conversation just continued.

Chat with the interviewer

Now, whenever I am interviewed, I do to the journalist what Rather did to me; I start a conversation in a low voice before the recording starts. I did that when Yang Lan, a famous talk show host in China, came by with a large entourage. We chatted. I asked how many people came with her. I asked how often she came to the United States and whether she had been to MIT before. I asked if anything had surprised her so far. When the cameras began to roll, I just raised my voice, and we carried on with the conversation we were already having.

Somewhere in there, Yang Lan and I are talking with each other about Artificial Intelligence. Ms. Yang is often called China's Oprah; I suspect in China, they refer to Oprah as America's Lan. Image courtesy of Adam Conner-Simons, MIT CSAIL.

Have a segue ready

You cannot anticipate everything you will be asked, and even if you could, there will be some questions you would rather not answer. You need to think about what to do in advance because you will not be able to work out what to do when the bright lights are shining on you. Here are some possibilities you could have ready to go:

- I haven't anything to say about that, so let's talk about....
- That question will be answered in time, but right now....
- Interesting question, but I think an even more interesting question is....
- I haven't focused on that because I think the real issue is....

For more possibilities, watch the way panelists answer questions about politics on the evening news.

Ask for the questions in advance

If your interviewer wants to extract thoughtful answers, not make you look stupid, your interviewer may be pleased to supply you with a few key questions in advance.

Once an interviewer told me he was planning to ask me why, for the past 50 years, AI researchers have been predicting computers would exhibit human-level intelligence within 20 years. I thought about that before the interview. Then, when asked, I said something like, "Oh well, let us forgive them because it will be true eventually. I think the real question is...." I could not have made that up on the spot.

What you need to know

Preparation increases the probability of interview success. Follow these steps:

- Anticipate likely questions. Prepare sensible, truthful answers.
- Show that you know about the institution and its people when you interview for a job.
- On camera, chat with the interviewer before the cameras begin to roll.
- Have a segue ready in case you do not want to answer a question.

The press is the best instrument for enlightening the mind of man, and improving him as a rational, moral and social being.

Thomas Jefferson; American statesman, diplomat, and third President

Communication from Thomas Jefferson to Thomas Cooper, 29 November 1802 (Lipscomb and Bergh, 1903–1904)

33 How to Write a Press Release

In this chapter, you learn what you need in a press release to increase the probability a busy journalist will look at it and then decide to use it. You also learn an important ordering principle.

Journalists are busy, so give them all they need

A journalist is a busy storyteller, and if you want a journalist to tell your story, you send in your story in the form of a press release that recognizes both the *busy* part and the *storyteller* part.

Some journalists receive hundreds of press releases each day. They do triage with a heavy hand, so you should be sure your press releases have the expected elements. In particular, press releases are expected to have the elements shown in the following template:

Your organization's name
Your organization's street address
Your organization's city, state, and zip code

Contact: *Your name*
Telephone: *Your telephone number*
Email: *Your email address*

> *When it is ok to publish your story*

HEADLINE

CITY, STATE, Date.

Your story

Your organization, what it does, and where it is.

Optionally, a picture.

         ##########

Write the story for them

You could write up a set of bullet points and leave it to the journalist to write the story:

Massachusetts Institute of Technology
77 Massachusetts Avenue
Cambridge, MA 02139

Contact: Clark Kent
Telephone: 617.253.1000
Email: superman@mit.edu

For Immediate Release

NEW PROGRAM IS IMPRESSIVE

CAMBRIDGE, MA, April 1, 1961.

- Program does symbolic integration.
- Written by James R. Slagle, a Ph.D. student.
- Slagle says it is impressive, solving most of the problems in a test set.

######### #

There would be no point in sending anyone such a press release. The headline is passive and boring, but worse yet, it leaves all the work of writing the story to the journalist, failing to recognize that journalists are busy.

Instead, your press release should be a draft story, to be used as is or with slight modification.

The following shows what a draft story might have looked like, back in 1961 when the work was done, announcing James Slagle's success in writing a program that solved calculus problems. Although based on a real achievement, the story, as written, is whimsical and contrived, so as to provide a starting point for discussion. The email address, postal code, and state abbreviation are modern.

Massachusetts Institute of Technology
77 Massachusetts Avenue
Cambridge, MA 02139

Contact: Clark Kent
Telephone: 617.253.1000
Email: superman@mit.edu

For Immediate Release

PROGRAM'S INTELLIGENCE EXCEEDS MIT FRESHMEN

CAMBRIDGE, MA, April 1, 1961. Julius A. Stratton, president of the Massachusetts Institute of Technology, announced that a graduate student in the Electrical Engineering Department, James R. Slagle, today demonstrated a program that solves problems in calculus at a level comparable to the very best students in freshmen calculus subjects. Slagle wrote the program to demonstrate that programs now have humanlike intelligence.

Professor Marvin Minsky, Slagle's thesis supervisor, expressed high praise for Slagle's work and its contributions to Artificial Intelligence: "This is the beginning of the end for us humans. If we are lucky, the machines may keep us as pets."

Slagle explained that the whole enterprise was easier than he expected: "I am fascinated by the way we humans transform hard problems into easier problems until the easier problems are so easy that the answers are obvious. We call it *problem reduction.*"

Once Slagle determined what he needed to do in general terms, it was just a matter of embedding the necessary transformations in his program, constructing a lookup table for the easy problems, and writing the computer code to apply the transforms and do the lookup. A few dozen transformations and 24 table entries sufficed.

In today's demonstration, Slagle's program solved 52 of the 54 hardest problems ever given to MIT students.

Slagle's problem-solving ideas will enable computers to solve a vast array of other problems.

The Massachusetts Institute of Technology (MIT) educates men and women of high potential through degree programs in engineering, science, business, architecture, and the humanities. MIT is located in Cambridge, Massachusetts.

##########

Expect your story to be trimmed

Your press release may arrive just as something is going to press. There is space to fill, but not enough to use your entire press release. Too bad, your journalist does not have time to trim and reorganize your press release.

That is why you adhere to an important maxim: Write a press release so that if a journalist draws a line between any two paragraphs, the material above the line is more important than the material below.

Focus on the headline

Your headline is the most important part of your press release. If it is exciting, your journalist may read more; if not, nothing else matters.

Many would find the following headline exciting because everyone is interested in whether computers can be truly intelligent. Note that there is an active verb, a *sine qua non* of excitement:

PROGRAM'S INTELLIGENCE EXCEEDS MIT FRESHMEN

Every time a computer program does something unexpected, a kind of hysteria sets in, and many think computers will soon take over. Knowing about this tendency, I think the sample headline lies on the wrong side of an ethical border because it suggests a program outperforms a group of people in general, not in a narrow domain. This is better:

PROGRAM SOLVES CALCULUS PROBLEMS

Include who, what, when, where, and why

Journalists are taught to be sure their stories answer five key questions. That is because a story that answers who, what, when, where, and why questions surely is a story. The sample press release does, in fact, answer the questions, and answers them all in the first paragraph.

Who
...James R. Slagle,...

What
...demonstrated a program that solves problems in calculus...

When
...today demonstrated a program that...

Where
...a graduate student in the Electrical Engineering Department,...

Why
Slagle wrote the program to demonstrate that programs now have humanlike intelligence.

Identify the VSN-C elements

If you are writing a piece about technical progress, you likely should be sure you have included the usual VSN-C elements. The sample press release does:

For more on VSN-C, see page 8.

Vision
I am fascinated by the way we transform hard problems into easier problems until the easier problems are so easy that the answers are obvious.

Steps
Once Slagle determined what he needed to do in general terms, it was just a matter of embedding the necessary transformations in his program, constructing a lookup table for the easy problems, and writing the computer code to apply the transforms and do the lookup.

News
In today's demonstration, Slagle's program solved 52 of the 54 hardest problems ever given to MIT students.

Contributions
Slagle's problem-solving ideas will enable computers to solve a vast array of other problems.

Include meaningful quotes

When you see someone quoted in a story, you know there is a human in the story, and that makes the story more interesting. The sample press release has two, and importantly, they introduce opinion and reflection, not data:

> Minsky: "This is the beginning of the end for us humans. If we are lucky, the machines may keep us as pets."

> Slagle: "I am fascinated by the way we humans transform hard problems into easier problems until the easier problems are so easy that the answers are obvious. We call it *problem reduction.*"

Minsky actually did make the crack about pets in an article written by Brad Darrach that appeared in *Life Magazine* (20 November 1970). Slagle actually did create the integration program while he was a graduate student at MIT, a milestone in Artificial Intelligence.

Details sell

Details make stories come alive. The sample press release offers, for example, these:

> We call it **problem reduction**.

> **A few dozen transformations and 24 table entries** sufficed.

> In today's demonstration, Slagle's program solved **52 of the 54 hardest problems** ever given to MIT students.

Exhibit excitement and passion

A press release can excite. Encourage the people you quote to express how exciting they find the news and that they show passion in their expression.

For more on showing passion, see page 157.

Purge acronyms and jargon from your story

Remember that even people in your field may not understand the acronyms and jargon you use with abandon, so abandon them. And note that when you use unfamiliar acronyms and jargon, you come across as elitist, thus making yourself unlikable.

Include a picture

Pictures, if used, provide detail, and pictures of people, like other kinds of details, make stories come alive.

Students at the Massachusetts Institute of Technology in Cambridge, MA. Image courtesy of Karen Prendergast.

Make your offering relevant

Know your journalist and what they cover. Do not annoy journalists by sending in material that they cannot possibly use. The sample press release would work for a computer journal, but not, for example, for the *Journal of Asphalt Paving Technologies*.

Know the rules of engagement

Most journalists are honorable people, and if one says a request will be honored, you can generally count on the request being honored. You should, however, make no assumptions. If you do not want your story to be published before some particular date, for example, make sure that the receiving organization honors the when-it-is-ok-to-publish-your-story line.

What you need to know

Journalists are storytellers. If they are to use your press release, the press release should be a draft that is as close as possible to what a journalist would write:

- Use a standard press-release template featuring elements that describe your organization, identify who can be sought out for more information and how, explain when it is permitted to publish the story, offer a headline, tell the story, describe what your organization does, and possibly offer a picture.
- Include a fantastically provocative headline.
- Honor the who, what, when, where, and why formula.
- Identify the Vision, Steps, News, and Contributions.
- Include quotes that express opinion or reflection.
- Remember that details sell.
- Be sure your story is relevant.
- Expect your story to be trimmed.
- Replace acronyms with their meanings.

34 How to Write a Review

In this chapter, you learn how to write a review of a paper or a book.

Evaluate the VSN-C elements

There are many kinds of reviews, including literature reviews. This chapter is about how to review a paper or a book. Such a review contains a summary, with details, plus your evaluation and your opinion about who should read the entire work.

You can use the standard Vision, Steps, News, and Contributions to shape your summary, but note that you have considerable artistic license with respect to which to include and where.

The following example, made up for illustration, reviews a paper written by Marvin Minsky. The K-lines paper, considered one of Minsky's seminal contributions, eventually appeared in *The Society of Mind* (Minsky, 1988):

> In his seminal work, *K-lines: A Theory of Memory*, Minsky suggests that if we are to understand human intelligence, we must answer four questions: How is information represented? How is it stored? How is it retrieved? And how is it used?
>
>   Minsky's answer is that the function of memory is to re-create a state of mind so that when confronted with a new problem, we can get back into the condition we were in when we previously solved a similar problem.
>
>   *K-line* is shorthand for *knowledge line*, a wirelike element that weaves its way among a pyramid of perceptual agents that process information coming up from below. Once sufficiently stimulated by actuated perceptual agents, a K-line puts other perceptual agents back into a previous state, hence re-creating a state of mind.
>
>   In further development of the theory, Minsky posits a pyramid of knowledge agents that mirrors the perceptual-agent pyramid. Actuated K-lines stimulate agents in the

Vision

Contribution

Step

Step

knowledge pyramid, which pass stimulation down to other knowledge-pyramid agents, which send stimulation via other K-lines back into the perceptual pyramid.

The K-line idea is among Minsky's greatest contributions to Artificial Intelligence. You should read this paper if you are interested in models of human problem solving.

Evaluation and who should read

Describe who should read what you have reviewed

Note that the Minsky review offers an opinion about who should read the paper. Whenever you think a work has merit, you should be specific about exactly who should read the entire work because the more a reader feels precisely described, the more likely the reader is to be persuaded.

Supply details

Because details sell, the following review I wrote for Rob Wesson's book, *Darwin's First Theory: Exploring Darwin's Quest for a Theory of Earth* (2017), mentions years, places, twisty roads, dead mussels, and potato fields:

News and evaluation

I knew Rob Wesson back when we were undergraduates at MIT. I was confident then that he would become an outstanding earth scientist, but I never asked myself if he would become an outstanding author. Now the evidence is in; he is.

Vision, expressed as the stories that needed to be told

Darwin's First Theory delights me in many ways: as a biography of Darwin focused on Darwin's life before he came to be an evolutionist, as an autobiographical account of Wesson's retracing of Darwin's geology-centered travels, and as a story of some of the people on the ground when the great Chilean earthquake of 2010 echoed the one in 1835 that so fascinated Darwin.

Contribution

Darwin was, like many, a little late in deciding what he wanted to do in his life, and experienced a bit of parental pressure in the direction of becoming a country parson. Then, he discovered a passion for geology, and worked up various theories, some right, and some wrong. Wesson describes all this with the skill of a first-class mystery writer, telling us early on enough to arouse curiosity, but not enough to guess how the story ends until the end.

Throughout, Wesson exposes the human side of how science worked back then, and still works today, describing Darwin's encounters with frustration, controversy, and occasional hard feelings.

Contribution

Wesson interleaves his Darwin story with descriptions of Wesson's own travels to examine the same geological features. Wesson gives us just the right amount of detail to make it all come alive, as if you yourself were bouncing along twisty roads, looking for places where lines of dead mussels tell tales of coastal uplift.

Steps

Read this book if you want to learn about how Darwin, one of the world's most important scientists, himself evolved. Read it if you want to get a glimpse of the human side of how science works. Read it if you are thinking of becoming a scientist. And read it if you are curious about how excited earth scientists get when they dig holes in potato fields, looking for layers of tsunami-deposited sand.

Who should read

What you need to know

A review of a paper or book should include standard elements with some essential extras:

- Include the standard Vision–Steps–News··· Contributions elements.

- Include your evaluation.

- Include a precise description of who should read the reviewed work.

- Include some details, because details sell.

He who praises everybody praises nobody.

Samuel Johnson; English poet, playwright, biographer, and lexicographer

From *The Works of Samuel Johnson, L.L.D: Together With His Life, And Notes on His Lives of the Poets, volume XI* (Johnson and Hawkins, 1787)

35 How to Write a Recommendation Letter

In this chapter, you learn essentials involved in recommending. You also learn about special cases: recommending someone for graduate admission, for an academic job, or for a scholarly prize.

Follow broadly applicable principles

You should, of course, use a VSN-C framework when you write a recommendation. You should also be careful to include additional essentials and exclude unintended elements that can reduce your influence.

For more on VSN-C, see page 8.

Include *Vision*, *Steps*, *News*, and *Contributions* elements

When writing a recommendation for someone—for admission, for a job, or for a prize—you are selling the candidate's competence, so your purpose is to establish that the candidate has a Vision and the characteristics needed to do something with the Vision. The character of the Vision varies, of course. A recommendation for admission to graduate school would focus on what the candidate wants to do and on the candidate's evident capabilities. A recommendation for a job would address outlook, skills, and momentum. A recommendation for a promotion or a prize requires emphasis on accomplishment, not potential.

Honor Grice's maxims

When recommending, you should honor community expectations. The British philosopher Paul Grice wrote about community expectations in communication, especially ordinary conversation, but the four maxims he discussed in the context of conversation make sense also in recommendations (Grice, 1989).

- The maxim of quality: In most communities, you are expected to tell the truth, so you should not lie. Similarly, you are expected to assert only that for which you have evidence, so you should not introduce speculations without identifying them as speculations.

- The maxim of quantity: You are expected to say what needs to be said, so you should be complete, supplying the level of detail your community expects.

- The maxim of relation: You are expected to be relevant, so you should not clutter up your communication with distractions.

- The maxim of manner: You are expected to be clear.

As Grice noted, if you appear to be violating one of the maxims deliberately, such a violation conveys implication. If your letter is too short, you violate the maxim of quantity and implicate a lack of enthusiasm. If you use ambiguous phrasing, you violate the maxim of manner and also implicate a lack of enthusiasm.

Write as much as the community expects

A colleague in Physics once told me he never wrote a tenure recommendation of more than one page. In his field, the community expectation is that recommendation letters rank the stars in a given subfield and assert where the candidate belongs in the list. In my field, Artificial Intelligence, a one-page letter would be viewed as unenthusiastic and negative. There is an expectation that enthusiastic recommenders go into considerable detail over the span of several pages.

Be unambiguous

A colleague came into my office and asked me to read a recommendation that he was drafting. I read it and said, "The letter seems unenthusiastic; is that want you want?" He was surprised and glad that he checked. I had noted that he had not actually written "...I recommend...."

So those words are a *sine qua non*, and once they are written, the question that emerges is which modifier do you use. None? With enthusiasm? With maximum enthusiasm? You have to choose carefully because the recommendation sentence will be read carefully and with much attempted interpretation.

The least ambiguous recommendation letter I ever read concluded this way: "If I have not convinced you to admit x, then I have not done my job. Let me know, and I will try harder."

Tell a story

When you include an interesting or amusing story about someone, you accomplish two objectives: first, it establishes that you actually do know the person fairly well, and second, it provides a kind of handle:

> When Dr. Rao first came to see me, as an undergraduate, I suggested he might work on a problem involving near-miss learning. "How," I asked, "might a learning program learn when no non-example is close to the learning program's evolving model?" I had been thinking about this for a few months without getting anywhere. To my astonishment, Dr. Rao came back two weeks later with a solution. "What have you been thinking about?" I asked. "Near-miss groups," he said, announcing the label for his elegant solution!

Use the candidate's title and surname

It is controversial, but when I recommend someone, I refer to them by surname. I want to be taken as objective and not so familiar with a candidate that I would refer to them by their given name, or even worse, by a diminutive name or nickname. Thus, at the beginning of a letter, I announce that I write to recommend Ms. Susan Competent or Mr. Patrick Competent, and then refer to Ms. Competent or Mr. Competent. I would never refer to Susan or Patrick, and I would heavily discount any recommendation in which the writer referred to her as Suzie or to him as Pat. I especially dislike Pat, which I take to be a unit of measure for butter.

Do not volunteer to be called

Many recommendations end with "Do not hesitate to call me...." Some readers assume this is code for "I'm not really keen on this candidate, but I don't want my fingerprints on a rejection, so call me and let me tell you how I really feel."

Of course, if you are truly unenthusiastic, perhaps you should not be writing at all. Tell the candidate you do not think you can write a letter that would be helpful.

Augment as needed in special cases

Beyond broadly applicable recommendation-writing principles lie specific needs for special cases.

For graduate admission, focus on evidence of research potential

Undergraduate admission is done by professionals whose goal is to build a balanced class. They are attracted to a mix of future poets, athletes, writers, scholars, entrepreneurs, and world savers.

Graduate admission is done by faculty whose goal is to enhance their research programs. They do not care about undergraduate activities unrelated to research, so do not dwell on such activities. A quick paragraph will make clear that the candidate has had a life, and even that may be of little interest.

Be particularly careful to avoid writing in a way that is influenced by gender. If you would not call a male candidate "charming," do not describe a female candidate that way.

For academic jobs, focus on Vision and progress

Jobs are offered because decision makers think the applicant will make their organization better. Universities, in particular, think in terms of improving short-term reputation. Thus, a candidate for a job must be a person who will have influence, and will have influence because of work done at the place that hires the candidate.

It follows that you should emphasize that the candidate is progressing on a series of steps toward a Vision and that important Steps are just ahead.

For business jobs, focus on recent achievement

Once someone has been in the workforce, nobody cares what happened before that. A job candidate may have been president of the undergraduate association or captain of the fencing team, but nobody cares unless you argue that those successes enable future success in some way. Employers want to know what a candidate can do for them.

If you are the candidate, you may want to keep your job search secret from your current employer, in which case you are likely to be your own chief recommender, with your résumé carrying much of the achievement you need to boast about. Focus your résumé on what you have just accomplished:

- Managed a project team of 25 engineers.
- Raised sales by 25% during the first year on the job.
- Developed a highly successful $25 million marketing campaign.

Also include a paragraph on your objectives with respect to the job you are seeking. Make sure that your objectives intersect with company success.

For prizes, focus on impact and inspiration

Prizes are awarded because the decision makers think the honored candidate will bring honor to the prize-awarding organization.

It follows that you need to assure the decision makers that choosing your candidate will be a wise decision. Then, it follows that a candidate for an award must have had influence.

Thus, you must explain influence. You can write about who was impressed and why; or who is working on next steps; or what places are using the ideas. All this helps to assure the decision makers that the world will respect their choice and not think they decided stupidly.

You can go one step further, and do better, by explaining the candidate's influence on you. Such an explanation assures the decision makers that choosing your candidate will be considered wise by at least one person. The following, for example, comes from a letter I wrote recommending Shimon Ullman for the Emit Prize for Science, Art, and Culture, which he won:

I have cited these particular examples of Dr. Ullman's work for two reasons: first, to lay out a few examples of Dr. Ullman's brilliant contributions, and second, to demonstrate, through the influence of those contributions on me personally, that the contributions reach far beyond the computer-vision community to researchers whose scientific passions center on the development of computational accounts of animal, and especially human, intelligence.

Ask for and provide talking points

If you agree to recommend someone, you should ask that person for a list of talking points. You should not have to dig a candidate's special qualities out of a cover letter, a statement of intent, or any sort of résumé.

If you are the candidate, your recommenders need your help. They always appreciate talking points, knowing that candidates often have special qualities that recommenders ordinarily would not know about.

Do not worry about seeming immodest in your talking points; your reviewer will adjust all the adjectives anyway.

What you need to know

If you agree to recommend someone for graduate admission, an academic job, or a scholarly prize, you should tell that person the degree to which your recommendation will be helpful. Then, in writing, you should adhere to the following principles:

- Be sure to identify the candidate's Vision, Steps, News, and likely Contributions.
- Be explicit and unambiguous as a courtesy to the readers.
- Avoid phrases interpretable as cautionary because they suggest deliberate ambiguity.
- Write as much as the community expects.

- Use the candidate's title and surname; avoid given names and, especially, diminutive names and nicknames.
- When you are the candidate, supply your recommenders with talking points.

If you recommend someone for graduate admission, then:

- Explain how the candidate will contribute to the research group the candidate proposes to join.

If you recommend someone for an academic job, then:

- Focus on the candidate's manifested Vision, Steps, News, and Contributions. Talk also about future Contributions that you foresee.

If you recommend someone for a business job, especially if the someone is yourself, you should adhere to the following:

- Focus on business achievements of interest to the readers.
- Focus on current work, not on earlier achievements.
- Mention degrees, but do not list activities not relevant to future work.

If you recommend someone for a prize, be sure to include this:

- Explain how the candidate has influenced you, especially if the influence was inspirational.

When I get ready to talk to people, I spend two thirds of the time thinking what they want to hear and one third thinking about what I want to say.

Commonly attributed to Abraham Lincoln; American statesman, lawyer, and 16th President

36 How to Run a Briefing Conference

In this chapter, you learn how to ensure that participants at a briefing conference are glad that they decided to be there and likely to be complimentary when they go home.

Be relevant

Briefing conferences introduce industrial participants to what is going on at the front lines of research. MIT's Industrial Liaison Program organizes industry-oriented briefing conferences three or four times each year in an effort to inform its member companies about MIT research developments and to discuss issues currently affecting their industries. Typically, each MIT ILP conference lasts a day or two and features presentations by leading MIT faculty and researchers as well as opportunities for informal discussions and socializing.

I worked with the ILP to run a briefing conference on *Reinventing Artificial Intelligence*. At the time, there were many skeptics—people spoke of an AI winter—so my purpose was to tell the world that spring had come.

The ILP people thought it was a good idea, so we decided to have a one-and-a-half-day affair with speakers from both MIT and industry.

Naturally, I was eager to see what it would take to ensure the conference was successful. Strangely, not many around MIT had thought about it, but those who had said to me, "Oh, you have to see Ira." Ira Alterman worked for a local company that sold carefully curated mailing lists, and Ira's company was often used by ILP to get brochures out to the right people.

So, I went to see Ira. "Ira, what do I need to do?" "Oh, it's easy, you just have to do two things," he said. "Make sure each talk ends with a slide titled *Business Messages* and make sure the participants get copies of all the slides."

Require a *Business Messages* slide

Why does each talk have to end with a slide titled *Business Messages*? Ira explained that academics often get so excited about the research they are doing, they forget that participants are going to be there to learn how they can use the new technology. If each talk ends with a slide titled *Business Messages*, it tells the participants there is, in fact, relevance to business.

And maybe more importantly, it forces the speakers to think about what business messages there are.

I concluded that a *Business Messages* slide functions as a special kind of Contributions slide, so I decided to pressure all the speakers into having a final slide titled *Business Messages*. I also added one to my introductory overview talk.

In an introductory overview, I finished with a *Business Messages* slide.

Business Messages
• AI is back
• Evidence from Microsoft, Disney, General Electric
• Hardware makes a difference
• It is not a one-idea field any more

My final slide noted that the entire conference demonstrated that AI had become important again; that there would be evidence offered by speakers from Microsoft, Disney, and General Electric, among others; that more powerful computers were enabling; and that the rule-based systems idea was no longer the only idea of real-world importance.

Give the participants copies of the slides

"Second," said Ira, "You need to be sure all the participants get copies of all the slides." This part seemed a little strange because I could not imagine how busy people would be spending time reviewing talks they had heard, but Ira seemed to know what he was talking about. Everyone was working on their slides right up to presentation time, but the moment they finished, I demanded copies of what they presented, had an assistant race off to a high-speed copy machine, and got copies to the 800 participants at each coffee break.

Note that I asked the speakers in advance if I could distribute their slides, and I suggested that they include on each slide a copyright notice or distribution limitation if they chose.

Identify the big ideas for the trip report

I thought things were going pretty well, so I went into our conference reception that evening feeling pretty good about the first day. But then, I asked one of the participants if he was enjoying the meeting. "Well," he said, "It's ok, but not as good as the conferences run by the Media Laboratory." Ugh. "Why is that?" I asked, hoping perhaps I could help him change his mind. "The Director of the Media Laboratory gets up from time to time and gives a good summary of the take aways."

The scales fell from my eyes. I suddenly realized why each talk had to end with a *Business Messages* slide; why the participants needed copies of all the slides; why I should give a summary of the big ideas from time to time.

The participants had to prepare trip reports when they got home.

I got up at 4:00 am, put together a big-messages presentation for the second morning, and delivered it just before the final coffee break of the meeting. I opened with, "MIT's President, Charles Vest, asked me to tell him the essentials of what has happened here. I'm not sure what you will tell your people back home, but here is what I will tell him, and by the way, I just made all these slides available for you on the web, along with all the business-messages slides. Feel free to adapt them to any purpose you may have."

Thus, I wrote up the slides for their trip report for them, or at least gave them a starting point that they could adjust to fit their own impressions. They seemed to appreciate it. When they filled out the conference evaluation during the ensuing coffee break, they gave it the highest score of any ILP conference ever.

What you need to know

Attention to a few essentials makes briefing conferences successful, especially those essentials that help the participants report on what happened.

- Provide copies of all briefing slides at some convenient point after the briefings.
- Require that each presentation conclude with a *Contributions* slide. If it is a briefing conference for business people, that contributions slide should be titled *Business Messages*.
- Summarize the big ideas, focusing on what you want attendees to remember.

37 How to Run a Panel Discussion

In this chapter, you learn how to ensure that a panel discussion works well. They usually do not, unnecessarily doomed by boring opening statements, long-winded introductions, and lack of moderator preparation.

Seat the panelists at three tables

The audience should feel they are witnessing a conversation that they are part of, not watching a boring sequence of unintelligible, hurried talks.

Conversations take place among four to six people, not more. You should seat them behind tables arranged in an open-U configuration. For the comfort of panelists, particularly if the panel is seated on a stage, make sure there is some kind of so-called modesty panel in front. The panelists need water to avoid drying out as well as pads of paper and pencils to work up what they want to say as the panel progresses.

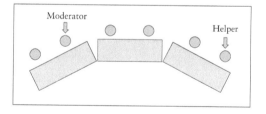

Shape matters. Arrange your panelists as if they were in a circle with the audience.

Note that you put the moderator at the table among the panelists, but not in the center or at the end. That helps create the feeling that the moderator is a part of the discussion.

Sometimes it helps to have an associate moderator; that way the associate moderator can think about the next set of questions while the moderator is busy working through a current set. Put the associate moderator at the end furthest from the moderator to keep him out of the center and to avoid inelegant symmetry.

Introduce the panel members briefly

As moderator, you should introduce the panel members. If you ask them to introduce themselves, they do not know what or how much to say. Limit your introductions to a sentence or two explaining why their opinions matter; if you say more, people in the audience will tune out.

Later, you can add useful detail about each panel member's products, work, and background in your questions:

- Marvin, during the years you worked on K-lines, did you ever...
- Patrick, having been Marvin's student, can you tell us...
- Susan, in your paper, x, why did you write that...

Forbid opening statements

At some point, someone will say: "Let's start the panel with opening statements, maybe give each panelist five minutes."

You should find a polite way to say that the five-minute part is a bad idea. Here is why: The participants will agonize over how to get their stump speeches into five minutes. They will fail. There will be too many slides. Each slide will have too many words. The talks will be unintelligible. The moderator will get nervous and start edging toward the front of his seat, hoping to get the speaker-who-never-quits to quit. Everything becomes tense. An hour can easily go by before the actual discussion starts.

Everyone should know better. In televised debates and town hall meetings, there are no opening statements with slides. At most, politicians get one minute or so to say something, which generally is not interesting.

It is better when the moderator simply asks questions that enable the speakers to say what they want to say. It looks like a spontaneous discussion.

For more on elevator pitches, see page 271. But what if you are a panelist and you get stuck with a moderator who wants opening statements? Start yours by saying, "I think it best if I do a short opening statement so we can get to questions and answers as soon as possible." Then give a relevant elevator pitch.

When I am on an opening-statement panel, I ask the moderator whether I can do the final opening statement. Then, I have the option of saying, "Well, time is moving fast, so I think it best if we skip my opening statement and just move right away to questions and answers. Let me start by asking myself the first question...."

Prepare the questions

There is another reason to avoid opening statements: it puts a burden on the panelists. Some may even be nervous about getting the opening statement right. That kills spontaneity.

You should, however, ask the panelists in advance what points they want to get across. Then, if you want to, you can ask them questions that will bring out those points as if they were spontaneous answers to questions.

Of course, you should also think about what points you want to get across and arrange to ask questions that will bring out those points.

Skip the lectern, get rid of the soft seating

Because there will be no opening statements and no slides, there should be no lectern. The last thing you want is for one of the panelists to spot one and then try to use it.

Avoid easy chairs of the sort you would find in a living room. The uninformed think they make the panelists look and feel comfortable; they do not. People sink into them, wondering what they look like from the audience. "Should I cross my legs?" "What do I do with my arms?" It just does not work.

Ask embarrassing questions, start arguments

Remember when you last watched a political debate. The moderators assume television viewers like to watch people squirm and fight. We are all voyeurs of a certain sort.

Ask a panelist why work is going so slowly. Ask a panelist why another panelist is wrong. Read goofy-in-retrospect quotes. Ask if there are grave dangers in what is being done.

Have the audience submit questions on cards

If the audience is large, you do not want microphones out there ready at hand for someone to ask a silly question, get long-winded, or take the panel where you do not want it to go. Have someone wander up and down periodically collecting questions written on cards; then you can sort them with a view toward asking the popular question or the best question or an amalgamating question. You can do this while your associate moderator is working through a set of questions.

Limit the discussion to an hour

You want the audience to wish there were more discussion, not wish there were less. An hour works well. Ninety minutes is generally too much. You need 90 minutes if there are opening statements, but you do not want opening statements.

Offer a summary when it is over

When the allotted time is up, you or a designated associate can tell people what they learned from the panel discussion. It is, of course, what you want them to learn.

Because you have prepared many of the questions and because you probably know the likely answers, you can prepare much of your summary in advance, making adjustments as interesting questions and answers emerge.

What you need to know

Panel discussions usually fail. To succeed, you should:

- Seat the panelists so that they can talk to each other.
- Work with an associate moderator to ensure flow.
- Skip the opening statements; introduce each speaker yourself, and then start up each speaker with a question.
- Prepare questions that stimulate debate and controversy.
- Get rid of the lectern and soft seating.
- Limit the discussion to an hour.

Sometimes I have good luck and write better than I can.

Commonly attributed to Ernest Hemingway; American journalist, novelist, and short-story writer

38 How to Write a Blog

In this chapter, you learn the characteristics that make blogs fun to write and fun to read.

Decide what kind of blog you are writing

You may write a blog because you want to persuade, in which case you should structure your blog writing with the Vision–Steps–News··· Contributions framework. You should include a Slogan, Symbol, Salient idea, Surprise, and Story.

For more on the VSN-C framework, see page 8.

For more on Winston's star, see page 21.

You may write a blog because you want to instruct, in which case you should start with an empowerment promise and conclude by delivering on your promise.

Your purpose may be neither to persuade nor to instruct but rather to tell a story. You may tell a story because you want to keep yourself or your organization in touch with friends, customers, alumni, or people who share your interests. You may tell a story because you want to review a service so as to compliment or criticize. You may tell a story because you enjoy engaging in a pleasurable, creative art form.

Tell a story with local color

We are truly storytelling animals. We love stories of all kinds, especially in blogs, which tend to tell stories about people and places that are funny or interesting or both.

For more on storytelling animals, see page 25.

Here is an excerpt from a what's-happening-at-our-place blog I wrote for *Slice of MIT*, the blog of the MIT Alumni Association, back when MIT was celebrating its 150th anniversary:

It came the old fashioned way, delivered by a mail carrier. "....I cordially invite you to a special luncheon ....Sincerely, Paul Gray." The price of admission was 50 years at MIT in one capacity or another.

I figured it would be an intimate affair, in one of the small dining rooms at the Faculty Club. Maybe 15 or 20 of us lifers would show up.

It turned out to be 150, and two or three had come to MIT before 1940, so 8,000 years is a conservative estimate of the experience present. If you lined those years up, you would get fairly close to when Cambridge was under an ice sheet.

Eventually, the lunch went open-microphone for reminiscences, and Professor Tony French recalled the very strange case of the daffodils.

It happened one day when Tony was new to MIT, teaching 8.01, freshman physics, in 26-100, our largest lecture hall. Part way into his lecture a trumpet sounded. Annoyed by the disruption, he scolded, "That will do," in the accent of the other Cambridge, and went on with his lecture.

A little later the trumpet sounded again, and a young woman, carrying a bunch of daffodils, but wearing only a top hat, bounded down the steps from the back of the hall, handed a daffodil to Tony, and departed.

"What would you have done?" Tony asked rhetorically. Tony himself decided to retire from the field for the rest of that day. This evidently led to considerable complaint from the students, who all demanded a refund for the loss of one hour of instruction.

Tell a story about what happened

A diary bores if all you do is report trips to the grocery store. Sometimes, however, something unusual happens, worth telling others about who might want to know what is happening or have a similar problem, especially if there are points of humor:

> **27 April:** I went out for my usual 3-to-5k, almost daily run, carefully avoiding all the roots and rocks on my

route through the woods. Then, I came home and, crash, tripped on a step. There was excruciating pain, but only for maybe 15 seconds.

It still hurt quite a bit to move during the next few days, especially getting up to a vertical position, but I wasn't too concerned when my health care provider said it would be more than two weeks before I could see a doctor.

I staggered over to my classes using my father-in-law's second-best walker and announced to my students I had a "sports-related injury," confessing that I tripped on a step. It seemed much less embarrassing, somehow, to speculate that it was a "sports-related injury," and because it happened right at the end of a run, Karen assured me there was a connection.

5 May: Just to be sure I had nothing more than strained quadriceps, I called my doctor's office, hoping I could get an appointment at least with a nurse. But then, I was granted a miracle: there was a cancelation; I could see a real live doctor!

My escort to the examination room asked what happened. "Oh, I strained my quads playing rugby," I said, followed immediately by "just kidding."

The examination didn't go well. The doctor poked around a little, seemed upset that he couldn't get a patellar reflex, and sent me to the emergency room.

When I got there, they wanted to know if I had chest pain. I said no and wanted to say I was anticipating a pain in another body part.

Curious onlookers kept looking at me in my ER cubicle. I later found that the rugby story had made it into the record, which the onlookers must have thought novel, in that I am no longer young.

I flunked a certain strength test, so I was scheduled for an MRI next day. I thought that would be like an X-ray. Maybe a few minutes to get set up and a second or two of beam. The operators thought it would take an hour a leg, but I was good at holding still so it only took an hour total. The machine sounded like a jackhammer most of the time.

Bad news: transected quadriceps tendons, both legs. Sounds bad. I prefer torn.

11 May, Surgery day: I showed up at noon and waited.

The anesthesiologist came by to discuss options. "You have two," he said, "general or spinal."

"What about the whiskey option," I said.

"Well, that used to be the only option, but we don't offer it any more. Not enough demand." I could see the day was going to be fun.

"Ok, I'll go for the spinal, that way I can supervise."

"Well, you won't do much supervising. We also give you a sedative, so you will be half asleep."

"Hmmm." I thought to myself. "It will be much like a faculty meeting. But still, I will have a sense of participation."

14 May: Someone came in and announced I was being transferred to the TCU. Ever suspicious, I wondered what that could be. My first guess was *Terminal Care Unit*. Whew, it turned out to be *Transitional Care Unit*.

18 May: A new nurse showed up. "How do you take your Miralax? Orange juice?"

"I don't always use Miralax, but when I do, I mix it into a glass of Dos Equis."

She looked at me funny. I guess she never saw the most-interesting-man-in-the-world ads.

And so on. *The Tale of Torn Tendons* diary blog kept my friends up to date, and writing it helped me maintain a positive attitude, looking for points of humor, for the four months it took to get completely back to normal and jogging again.

Write a review, especially if positive

Many internet reviewers have their guns loaded, deriving satisfaction from finding ways to fire away at anything or anyone. You can help make the world a better place if you not only write against what deserves to be condemned but also put some time into complimenting what you like. I recommend a ratio of three or more positive reviews for every negative review.

In the following example, the review tells a story about a vacation day in Venice. The writer, Karen Prendergast, is about as positive as can be. Note that she included pictures. Pictures supply details. Details sell.

A Great Day at The Gritti Epicurean School

Our party of four signed up for a half-day cooking class with Chef Franco Sanna at The Gritti Epicurean School because we wanted to learn more about Venetian cuisine. We had read good things about the class, but we were not prepared for how amazing our day with Chef Sanna would be. The experience far exceeded our expectations in every possible way.

We met Chef Sanna in the lobby of The Gritti Palace promptly at 9:00 am and set off on foot at a brisk pace for the Rialto market, while he explained a bit about his background and asked us about our backgrounds and cooking experiences and about our food allergies and preferences. When we arrived at the market, Chef Sanna did a quick reconnaissance tour, looking at the offerings at several fish stalls and at several fruit and vegetable stands. Then he gathered us off to one side and told us what he thought looked exceptionally good that morning and scribbled out a menu, making sure we were happy with each dish he planned we would make.

Next, seeing that we were fish-buying neophytes, he explained the qualities he looked for when buying different types of seafood at the market, and pointed out fish that he would happily purchase and fish he would never purchase.

When it was time to purchase a whole fish to cook, Chef Sanna went to the fish monger he determined had the best fish that day and asked him to display the fish to us, showing us the bright gills and eyes, asking us to smell the fresh ocean (not fishy) smell, and having us touch the flesh to feel how firm it was, before the fish monger cleaned and wrapped the fish for us.

We thought picking out the fruits and vegetables would be pretty easy because there were so many beautiful choices, we couldn't possibly go wrong. Chef Sanna saw what we hadn't noticed and explained why he would buy only certain items from one vendor and certain items from another.

Just as we were finishing our purchases, the first groups of tourists began to arrive at the market, so we headed to Cantina do Mori for a few plates of cicchetti and glasses of prosecco. Now fortified, we headed back to The Gritti Palace, stopping briefly along the way at Cibo to pick up some cheese.

When we returned to the hotel, Chef Sanna brought us into the cooking school kitchen, which is extremely well-designed with incredible equipment and a huge table for serving the meal, handed us our aprons, and put us to work.

Well, actually, one of us did lots of work, including cutting up the fish. Three of us helped a bit but mostly watched and took lots of pictures while Chef Sanna performed his magic, creating three incredible dishes with multiple layers of flavor in about three hours (but certainly repeatable at home probably in a lot more time). And, unlike a magician, Chef Sanna happily shared his tricks.

We had a remarkable lunch, course by course with Chef Sanna at the big table in the center of the room, where we chatted about Venice, cooking, and how wonderful the lunch was. The ingredients were superb, and the cooking techniques were direct, so the flavors could shine. The sommelier served interesting local wines with each course, while singing gondolieri floated by the windows overlooking the canal. It was a perfect day!

What you need to know

We humans love stories. Popular blogs generally tell good stories.

- Tell stories in which you are involved that are funny or amazing.
- Tell stories about your place that are funny or amazing.
- Include details. Details sell.
- Include dialogue. Dialogue makes stories feel real.
- Include pictures. Pictures supply detail. Details sell.

There it is.

Frequent remark of Joseph II, Holy Roman Emperor

From *Amadeus*, a film directed by Milos Forman
for Orion Pictures, 1984

Epilogue: You Are Empowered

I opened this book with an empowerment promise:

> You will learn how to speak and write well from this book. The return on the time you invest in acquiring knowledge about how to communicate will be bigger than the return on any other investment you make.

Now it is time to deliver on that promise by noting how you have become empowered:

- You learned essentials of persuasion, including the Vision–Steps–News··· Contributions way of structuring communications and various ways of making communications memorable.
- You learned essentials for instruction, including the empowerment-promise way of structuring instruction.
- You learned ideas specific to presentation, with emphasis on slide composition.
- You learned ideas specific to writing, with emphasis on organization and style.
- You learned about instruction, especially the role of stories.
- You learned about design, especially layout.
- You learned about special cases, from poster construction to blog writing.

As you read, you learned a total of 246 communication facts, rules, and principles you need to know, all identified in each chapter's *What you need to know* section. You will not use all of those suggestions all the time. Some may not suit you. Some you may think wrong. But remember what you read in the Prologue:

> If you make use of just one principle from reading this book, that principle may be the life-changing one that gets you the job, wins the award, brings in the grant or contract, makes the sale, convinces your boss, excites the venture capitalist, inspires a student, or starts a revolution.

You have been empowered. Use your power wisely.

Patrick Henry
Winston preparing
for his 2019 *How to
Speak* talk in the
Center of the
Universe. Image
courtesy of Karen
Prendergast.

Bibliography

Harold Abelson, Don Allen, Daniel Coore, Chris Hanson, George Homsy, Thomas F. Knight Jr., Radhika Nagpal, Erik Rauch, Gerald Jay Sussman, and Ron Weiss. Amorphous computing. *Communications of the Association for Computing Machinery*, 43(5):74–82, May 2000.

Lorin W. Anderson and David R. Krathwohl, editors. *A Taxonomy for Learning, Teaching, and Assessing: A Revision of Bloom's Taxonomy of Educational Objectives*. Allyn and Bacon, 2001.

Hiba Awad. Culturally based story understanding. Master's thesis, Electrical Engineering and Computer Science Department, Massachusetts Institute of Technology, Cambridge, MA, 2013.

Ken Bain. *What the Best College Teachers Do*. Harvard University Press, 2004.

Scott Berkum. *Confessions of a Public Speaker*. O'Reilly Media, 2010.

Robert C. Berwick and Noam Chomsky. *Why Only Us*. MIT Press, 2016.

B. S. Bloom, M. D. Engelhart, E. J. Furst, W. H. Hill, and David R. Krathwohl, editors. *Taxonomy of Educational Objectives: The Classification of Educational Goals, Handbook 1: Cognitive Domain*. David McKay Company, 1956.

Cynthia Breazeal. *Designing Sociable Robots*. MIT Press, 2001.

Rodney Brooks. Intelligence without representation. *Artificial Intelligence*, 47(1-3):139–159, 1991.

Lewis Carroll. *Alice's Adventures in Wonderland*. Wisehouse Classics, 2017.

Julia Child, Louisette Bertholle, and Simone Beck. *Mastering the Art of French Cooking: Volume One*. Alfred A. Knopf, 1971. Twentieth printing.

Winston S. Churchill. *A Roving Commission: My Early Life*. Charles Scribner's Sons, 1930.

Winston S. Churchill. This was their finest hour, 18 June 1940. Speech to House of Commons, London. Text and audio available from International Churchill Society website: https://winstonchurchill.org/resources/speeches/1940-the-finest -hour/their-finest-hour/.

Winston S. Churchill. *The Second World War*. Houghton Mifflin Company, 1948 to 1953. Six volumes.

Lewis Copeland and Lawrence W. Lamm, editors. *The World's Greatest Speeches*. Dover Publications, 1973. Speech by Patrick Henry, Give me liberty or give me death, to Second Virginia Convention, St. John's Church, Richmond, VA, 23 March 1775. From William Wirt, Sketches of the Life of Patrick Henry, 1836.

Brad Darrach. Meet Shaky, the first electronic person: the fascinating and fearsome reality of a machine with a mind of its own. *Life Magazine*, page 68, 20 November 1970.

W. Edwards Deming. *Out of the Crisis*. MIT Center for Advanced Engineering Study, 1986.

Nancy Duarte. *slide:ology: The Art and Science of Creating Great Presentations*. O'Reilly Media, 2008.

Lyn Dupré. *BUGS in Writing: A Guide to Debugging Your Prose*. Addison-Wesley, second edition, 1998.

Albert Einstein. On the electrodynamics of moving bodies. *Annalen der Physik*, 322(10):891–921, 1905.

Dwight D. Eisenhower. *Public Papers of the Presidents of the United States, Eisenhower 1957: containing the public messages, speeches, and statements of the president, January 1 to December 31*. Office of the Federal Register, National Archives and Records Administration, 1957. Remarks to the National Defense Executive Reserve Conference, Washington, DC, 14 November 1957. Text available at: https://quod.lib.umich.edu /p/ppotpus/4728417.1957.001/857.

Peter Elbow. *Writing Without Teachers*. Oxford University Press, second edition, 1998.

Ralph Waldo Emerson. Self-reliance. In Joseph Slater, Alfred R. Ferguson, and Jean Ferguson Carr, editors, *The Collected Works of Ralph Waldo Emerson (Essays: First Series)*. Harvard University Press, 1979. Essay written in 1841.

Harold Evans. *Do I Make Myself Clear?: Why Writing Well Matters*. Little Brown, 2017.

Rae Ann Fera. Annie Leibovitz on getting the shot and the future of photography. *Fast Company*, 28 June 2013. URL: https://www.fastcompany.com/2683295/annie-leibovitz-on-getting-the-shot-and-the-future-of-photography.

Stephen Frantzich. *Honored Guests: Citizen Heros and the State of the Union*. Rowman and Littlefield Publishers, 2011.

Carmine Gallo. *Talk Like TED: The 9 Public-Speaking Secrets of the World's Top Minds*. Saint Martin's Griffin, 2015.

David Gordon. Vocal warmup tongue twisters, 2016. URL: http://www.spiritsound.com/twisters.html.

Jonathan Gottschall. *The Storytelling Animal: How Stories Make Us Human*. Houghton Mifflin Harcourt, 2012.

Ulysses S. Grant. *Personal Memoirs of Ulysses S. Grant*. Charles L. Webster & Company, 1885. Modern edition published in 1994 by Smithmark Publishers Inc., by special arrangement with W. S. Konecky Associates, Inc.

H. Paul Grice. *Studies in the Way of Words*. Harvard University Press, 1989.

Linda Hermer-Vazquez, Elizabeth Spelke, and Alla S. Katsnelson. Sources of flexibility in human cognition: Dual-task studies of space and language. *Cognitive Psychology*, 39(1):3–36, 1999.

Samuel Johnson and John Hawkins. *The Works of Samuel Johnson, LL.D.: Together With His Life, And Notes on His Lives of the Poets*, volume XI. Printed for J. Buckland and 40 others, 1787.

Karen Kelsky. *The Professor Is In: The Essential Guide to Turning Your Ph.D. into a Job*. Three Rivers Press, 2015.

John Fitzgerald Kennedy. Inaugural address, 20 January 1961. Speech to the Nation, Washington, DC. Text and video are available at the John F. Kennedy Presidential Library and Museum website, URL: https://www.jfklibrary.org/learn/about-jfk/historic-speeches/inaugural-address.

Alex Krizhevsky, Ilya Sutskever, and Geoffrey E. Hinton. Imagenet classification with deep convolutional neural networks. In F. Pereira, C. J. C. Burges, L. Bottou, and K. Q. Weinberger, editors, *Advances in Neural Information Processing Systems 25*, pages 1097–1105. Curran Associates, Inc., 2012.

James M. Lang. *Small Teaching: Everyday Lessons from the Science of Learning.* Jossey-Bass, 2016.

Andrew A. Lipscomb and Albert E. Bergh, editors. *The Writings of Thomas Jefferson, Memorial Edition, 20 volumes.* Thomas Jefferson Memorial Assocation of the United States, 1903–1904. URL: https://famguardian.org/Subjects/Politics/Thomas Jefferson/jeffbibl.htm.

Andrew Lo. *Adaptive Markets: Financial Evolution at the Speed of Thought.* Princeton University Press, 2017.

Kingsley Martin. Winston Churchill interviewed in 1939: The British people would rather go down fighting. *New Statesman*, 19 December 2013. Reprinted from the 7 January 1939 issue of *New Statesman Magazine.*

James McPherson. *Battle Cry of Freedom.* Oxford University Press, 1988.

Charles-Joseph Minard. Tableaux graphiques et cartes figuratives, 1869. Bibliothèque numérique patrimoniale des ponts et chaussées, accessed 2019-08-11. URL: https://patrimoine .enpc.fr/document/ENPC01_Fol_10975.

Marvin Minsky. Steps toward artificial intelligence. *Proceedings of the IRE*, 49(1):8–30, 1961.

Marvin Minsky. K-lines: a theory of memory. *Cognitive Science*, 4:117–133, 1980.

Marvin Minsky. *The Society of Mind.* Simon and Schuster, 1988.

Marvin Minsky. *The Emotion Machine.* Simon and Schuster, 2006.

Josef Müller-Brockman. *Grid systems in graphic design.* Niggli, 2017.

Anh Nguyen, Jason Yosinsky, and Jeff Clune. Deep neural networks are easily fooled: High confidence predictions for unrecognizable images. *arXiv:1412.1897*, 2014.

Andrea Palladio. *The Four Books of Architecture (Dover Architecture Book 1)*. Dover Publications, 1965.

Plato. *The Republic*. Xist Publishing, 2016. Written 380 BCE.

Sajit Rao. *Visual Routines and Attention*. PhD thesis, Electrical Engineering and Computer Science Department, Massachusetts Institute of Technology, Cambridge, MA, 1998.

Ronald Reagan. Remarks on East-West relations, 12 June 1987. Speech at the Brandenburg Gate, West Berlin. Text available at Ronald Reagan Presidential Library & Museum website, URL: https://www.reaganlibrary.gov/research/speeches/061287d.

Garr Reynolds. *presentationzen: Simple ideas on Presentation Design and Delivery*. New Riders, second edition, 2012.

Sam Roberts. The elements of style turns 50. *The New York Times*, 22 April 2009.

Emil Ruder. *Typographie*. Verlag Niggli, 1967.

Faria Sana, Tina Weston, and Nicholas J. Cepeda. Laptop multitasking hinders classroom learning for both users and nearby peers. *Computers & Education*, 62:24–31, 2013.

William Shakespeare. The Tragedy of Hamlet, Prince of Denmark, 1600. URL: opensourceshakespeare.org/views/plays/playmenu .php?WorkID=hamlet, Act III, Scene 2, Lines 1950–1952.

Claude E. Shannon. A mathematical theory of communication. *The Bell System Technical Journal*, 27:379–423; 623–656, 1948.

William Strunk and E. B. White. *The Elements of Style*. Macmillan, fourth edition, 2014. First edition, 1959; Fiftieth anniversary edition, Pearson Longman, 2009.

Ivan E. Sutherland. Technology and courage. In Richard F. Rashid, editor, *CMU Computer Science: A 25th Anniversary Commemorative*. Association for Computing Machinery Press, 1991.

Ian Tattersall. *Becoming Human*. Harcourt, 1998.

Ian Tattersall. Human evolution and cognition. *Theory in Biosciences*, 123(4):371–379, 2010.

Ian Tattersall. *Masters of the Planet: the search for our human origins*. Palgrave, Macmillan, 2012.

Ian Tattersall. At the birth of language. *The New York Review of Books*, 2016.

Owen Thomas. Apple: Hello, iPhone. *CNN Money*, 9 January 2007. URL: money.cnn.com/2007/01/09/technology/apple_jobs/.

Edward R. Tufte. *The Visual Display of Quantitative Information*. Graphics Press, 2001. Second edition.

Edward R. Tufte. *The Cognitive Style of PowerPoint: Pitching Out Corrupts Within*. Graphics Press, 2006.

Alan M. Turing. Computing machinery and intelligence. *Mind*, 59(236):433–460, 1950.

Shimon Ullman. *High-Level Vision*. MIT Press, 1996.

Oriol Vinyals, Alexander Toshev, Samy Bengio, and Dumitru Erhan. Show and tell: A neural image caption generator. *Cornell University Library, arX.org>cs>arXiv:1411.4555*, 2014.

Celia Walden. In my job, it's just like being a man—but better. *The Telegraph*, 20 October 2013. URL: https://www.telegraph.co.uk/culture/tvandradio/10392498/Christiane-Amanpour-In-my-job-its-just-like-being-a-man-but-better.html.

James Watson. *The Molecular Biology of the Gene*. W.A. Benjamin, 1965.

James Watson and Francis Crick. A structure for deoxyribose nucleic acid. *Nature*, 171(4356):737–739, 1953.

Rob Wesson. *Darwin's First Theory: Exploring Darwin's Quest for a Theory of Earth*. Pegasus, 2017.

Patrick Henry Winston. *Learning structural descriptions from examples*. PhD thesis, Electrical Engineering Department, Massachusetts Institute of Technology, Cambridge, MA, 1970.

Patrick Henry Winston. *Artificial Intelligence*. Addison-Wesley, first edition, 1977. Third edition published in 1992.

Patrick Henry Winston. *Artificial Intelligence*. Addison-Wesley, third edition, 1992. First edition published in 1977.

Patrick Henry Winston. The strong story hypothesis and the directed perception hypothesis. In Pat Langley, editor, *Technical Report FS-11-01, Papers from the AAAI Fall Symposium*, pages 345–352, Menlo Park, CA, 2011. AAAI Press.

Patrick Henry Winston. Model-based story summary. In Mark A. Finlayson, Ben Miller, Antonio Lieto, and Remi Ronfard, editors, *Proceedings of the 6th Workshop on Computational Models of Narrative (CMN 2015)*, volume 45. Open Access Series in Informatics (OASics), Schloss Dagstuhl–Leibniz-Zentrum fuer Informatik, Dagstuhl, Germany, 2015.

Patrick Henry Winston. Self-aware problem solving. MIT DSpace, Computational Models of Human Intelligence Community, CMHI Report Number 2, Massachusetts Institute of Technology, 2018. URL: http://hdl.handle.net/1721.1/119652.

Patrick Henry Winston and Dylan Holmes. The Genesis Enterprise: Taking artificial intelligence to another level via a computational account of human story understanding. MIT DSpace, Computational Models of Human Intelligence Community, CMHI Report Number 1, Massachusetts Institute of Technology, 2018. URL: http://hdl.handle.net/1721.1/119651.

David P. Womersley, editor. *The Life of Samuel Johnson, LL.D. by James Boswell*. Penguin Classics, 2008. *The Life of Samuel Johnson, L.L.D.* was originally published by James Boswell in 1791.

Index

Colophon

I created this book using XeLaTeX, a typesetting system much like LaTeX but with more support, at the time of printing, for working with type families. XeLaTeX and LaTeX are descendents of TeX, Donald Knuth's computer typesetting system.

Knuth has said he started thinking about computer typesetting after looking at the first edition of my textbook on Artificial Intelligence (Winston, 1977), which was one of the earliest books typeset by the author of the book.

XeLaTeX, LaTeX, and TeX are often rendered as X$_{\exists}$L^{A}T$_{E}$X, L^{A}T$_{E}$X, and T$_{E}$X.

The principal type family is Sabon LT Std, and the body type is Sabon LT Std Regular. Headings are set in Frutiger.